SUPERSTAR SEASONALS

*18 Proven-Dependable Futures Trades
For Profiting Year After Year*

by
John L. Momsen

Published by
Windsor Books
P.O. Box 280
Brightwaters, NY 11718

Printed in the United States

ISBN 978-0-930233-72-3

To my wife,

Maryann

TABLE OF CONTENTS

INTRODUCTION

My name is John Lawrence Momsen. I've been a trader since 1974 and a full time trader since 1983. Trading is my business. Writing is my hobby. In 1998, I wrote my first book *Ultra-Reliable Seasonal Trades*. The sales were excellent, and I received many compliments on the accuracy of the trades and the ease of reading and understanding my methods. *Superstar Seasonals* is an expansion of my first book. It contains 18 trades – nine completely new trades and nine revisions from the trades in my first book. As in my first book, I have labored to make each and every trade easy to understand and easy to use.

You'll not find any crazy Greek letters nor any complicated formulas that can only be comprehended by a graduate student in Mathematics. Simplicity is my main trading style, and simple is the way I like to keep my life.

In Chapter 1, I'll introduce new seasonal traders to the concept of seasonal trading. And I'll also discuss a new type of seasonal I've discovered. This seasonal is not based solely on the direction of the move but on the strength and volatility of a potential move. I've nicknamed this a "Volatile Seasonal." This seasonal is designed to not only capture profits from normal seasonal trades but to profit from counter-seasonal trends that may develop. Many of these counter-seasonal trends prove to be far more profitable than ordinary seasonals.

Chapter 2 is about the importance of combining a winning trading system with a seasonal tendency. I'll walk you through the day-to-day operations of two trades and show you just how easy my Mega-Seasonal Method is to work with. By the way, you don't need an expensive computer or even an inexpensive calculator - just a pencil and some paper.

After talking with readers of *Ultra-Reliable Seasonal Trades*, I realized that money management was sadly lacking in most of their market training. In

Chapter 3, I'll share with you my simple money management system (I've named "SUMM") to aid in your trading education. I've also discovered a unique visual method to correlate the future profitability of seasonal trades. It's something I've never read about in other trading books. It's designed specifically to judge the historical strength of a seasonal.

Chapters 4 through 16 outline each of the 18 seasonal trades. In Chapter 4 you'll notice I've put brief explanatory comments next to each of the sections which appear in all of the trade presentations throughout the book. Though some of the sections are largely self-explanatory, I've still put in explanatory comments for all sections regardless. This is just to make things crystal clear for everyone, including novice traders. Each trade has a section for Fundamental Information, Past Performance History, a seasonal chart, Trade Rules and up to 42 years of trade-by-trade information. Also each section has comments about the trade, i.e. – what are the fundamentals behind the trade, what to watch for in a chart set-up, what to expect during the trade and how and when the trade bottoms or tops out. Even if you eventually decide to design your own trading method, the information in these chapters will be of invaluable importance.

Lastly, Chapter 17 contains a visual dictionary of chart patterns that I've mentioned throughout the book.

At the end of the book I've included a calendar of "Entry Time Windows." This simplifies month-to-month trading and alerts you to the trades that are currently active. I hope you enjoy this book and it adds to your trading education. Remember, futures trading is an ongoing education. There's an old phrase in trading and in life, "If you snooze, you lose!" Keep your eyes open and your chin up. You can make money trading futures!

- Chapter 1 -

SEASONALS AND MEGA-SEASONALS

Many professional traders use seasonals as one of their basic trading methods. What are seasonals, why do they exist, how can they be identified and how can I use them? These are some of the questions novice traders ask, and I shall attempt to answer, in this chapter.

First, seasonals, what are they? In "The Microsoft Encarta Dictionary" one definition of the word "season," from which the word seasonals comes, is: "a period of the year marked by something such as a particular activity or the availability of a particular food." No definition could be more appropriate for the seasonal trader. There are times of the year when certain functions must be done. Very often this time is spread over a narrow time frame. Simple examples of this include the planting, the growing and the harvesting of crops, and the normal increase or decrease in demand for certain products, i.e. – petroleum products. Often these seasonal tendencies are driven by the nature of the weather conditions in the growing areas of certain crops. These conditions are usually the strongest driving force behind the seasonal crop trade. After all, weather conditions can't be changed. They may vary from time to time, but they are pretty much a fixed part of nature.

The next question is: "Why do these seasonal conditions exist?" As I've just stated, nature (and not man) controls these conditions. Another version of the question might be: "Why do these seasonal conditions exist in the commodity markets?" Of course the answer is simple. They exist because man has not yet conquered nature as far as growing cycles or weather cycles is concerned.

Many non-believers in seasonal trading argue that over time seasonal trades disappear. They believe that as traders notice the existence of a seasonal tendency, a great number of them will take positions in the markets waiting for the seasonal move to begin. The next part of their theory suggests that after everyone acquires a position, there will be no one left to enter the market to spur on the price move in the seasonal direction. There are a couple of problems with this theory.

First, as the traders enter the market on the seasonal side, they will begin the price change that is indicated by the seasonal trend. Second, and very possibly the most important reason, is that not all traders are trading the market in the same way.

The market is made up of many traders, each with their own style of trading. Yes, there are seasonal traders. Yet there are also day traders, swing traders, momentum traders, and spread traders, among others. Plus, a very large percentage of "traders" are commercials. The commercials are not trading solely to make a profit in the futures market. Unlike the speculator, commercials have the actual product to buy or sell. These commercials, such as farmers, may take the other side of the seasonal trade because they need to sell the product and lock in a profit. Other commercials, users, may take a seasonal trade because they need the commodity to fuel their factories and get their end product to market.

Quite often these buyers are not only concerned with the commodity's actual price. I'm sure you've seen news reports stating that only about three cents of the price of a loaf of bread goes to the farmer. This is approximately correct. So the buyer for the bakery is far less concerned with the price of the wheat that goes into his product than other costs such as labor, utilities, etc. He's got to keep his people working, and he's got to keep his clientele supplied. In this case the price of wheat is of little consequence.

The next question: "How are seasonal commodity trades identified?" The first step is the creation of a chart. This helps to visualize the potential seasonal trade. To create a chart I set up a very large spreadsheet. Each row across contains the closing price for the same month and day of the total years studied. Each column down contains all the data for each individual year studied. All of the closes for each individual year are then totaled and an average computed. This average is the average price for the year. Each daily close is then divided by this yearly average. This converts each daily close to a percentage of the average yearly price.

As an example, let's say that the year's average price for December 2000 Corn is $2.50. And the close for September 9, 2000 is $2.00. The computed index number for that day is 80% ($2.00 divided by $2.50). Then all of the data for all September 9ths is added and averaged to come up with an overall average for September 9ths. This is done for every trading day of the year. These numbers are then strung together to form a chart like the one below. Notice that the bottom of the chart shows the month. The left side shows the index number. Please don't confuse this index number with a price. As I said, the number is actually a percentage of the average price for the commodity for the year.

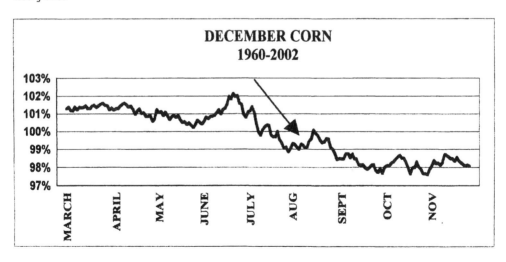

There is a debate in the industry about the number of years' data that should be used. Some believe that by using only the last 15 years of daily data you can visualize the seasonal trend and have the most recent information. Others believe that you should use all of the data you have available. I believe more in the longer term than the shorter term. After all, when average weather conditions change they change very slowly. Furthermore, I have noticed that some seasonals that appear in 15-year charts disappear in the longer term chart.

This was made quite clear to me one day when I was contacted by a reader of my first book. He e-mailed me with a 100% sure thing orange juice trade. He wrote that it had been profitable for each of the last 15 years and asked me to check through my much larger database to see how it would have worked prior to the most recent 15-year period.

I did as asked, since I'm always looking for new seasonal trades. Boy, was I surprised with the results. Yes, it had been profitable for each of the last 15 years – a perfect record. Yet, surprisingly, I found that it had been just as UN-perfect for the previous 15 years. Almost every one of the early years had been losers.

This obviously wasn't the new seasonal I was looking for. However, it did signal a potential problem for designing a seasonal chart. You see, the 30-year chart still seemed to exhibit the seasonal. I thought about a way to correct this and came up with a new theory of seasonal chart design. Instead of using only one chart that contained all the data I had in my database, I built multiple charts, each containing only a section of the total data. Basically, if I had data stretching back to 1960 and up through 2002, the first chart would contain only data from 1960 through 1974 (a 15-year period). The next chart would contain data from 1961 through 1975. And the third chart would contain data from 1962 through 1976. Each 15-year chart moving forward one year. Then after all the charts were built, I compared them.

Sure enough, the orange juice charts showed the possible change in the seasonal. This change was more than enough evidence that the seasonal might not be real, and would be one that I would choose not to trade. Before I included a single-directional seasonal trade in this book, I recreated this research time and time again. You can be assured that each of the single-direction trades have passed this visual test.

However, some of the trades in the book are multidirectional, meaning that the trade enters on either side of the market depending upon the price action. In these trades I look not for the repeated direction of the seasonal tendency, but for the repeated size and strength of the move. These trades usually take place around the growing stages of certain crops. They are driven by the prevailing weather conditions at the time and are quite often the most profitable seasonal trades.

Now for the most important question: "How can I use seasonals in my trading?" This question is so important that I've dedicated the whole next chapter to my answer.

- Chapter 2 -

TRADING WITH THE
MEGA-SEASONAL SYSTEM

The usual method for trading seasonals is what I call "buy on X and sell on Y." In other words, most seasonal traders use a simple date entry and date exit system. This is the system most seasonal trading manuals promote. It is easy to understand and makes the complicated job of successfully trading commodities simple.

As far as I'm concerned, though, this approach is way too risky for my trading capital. Anything can happen between the entry and exit dates, and often does. While by exit time you may make a profit, you might actually have to risk your total account on one seasonal trade if that trade goes far against your position.

This is the reason I designed *The Mega-Seasonal Trading System*. It lets the prevailing market action activate an entry for the seasonal. This system has a protective stop so that you can limit the risk on your trading capital. It also has a trailing profit stop to protect some of the paper profits you have earned in the trade, in the event of a change in the trend direction.

The basic design of *The Mega-Seasonal Trading System* is a simple breakout method, much like the legendary and fabulously profitable Turtle Trading System is rumored to be founded upon. In fact, this long-term trend following system was an inspiration for me, and actually helped draw me into the world of seasonals. I would develop simple trading systems along similar lines for various commodities and make a list of the trades, both profitable and non-profitable, on a calendar. It didn't take long to see that most of the large profit trades each year were entered during the same time period and exited during the same time period.

This shouted out seasonal trades! As I investigated further into the seasonal fundamentals of the various commodities, I was happy to discover that my initial reasoning about the winning trades was correct. A majority of the big winners happened at the time of the year when certain seasonal considerations were in force. Of course, not all the trades made during this time period were profitable, and there were profitable trades outside of the time window. Adding seasonal time frames to my trading systems took care of one of the biggest problems with long-term trend following systems - a large number of losses in a row resulting in a fairly large drawdown of capital. Like every other trader out there, my basic trust in my trading system would ebb and flow depending upon the latest trades. I have read a study commissioned by the Chicago Board of Trade stating that the average trader begins to lose faith in his trading system after three losing trades in a row. The degree to which this generalization holds true naturally depends upon the experience of the trader. It also depends upon the trader's personal discipline. This discipline, or lack of it, can make or break a trader.

That is another reason for adding seasonal time frames to my trend following systems. Personally, I was one of those traders who began to get nervous if I seemed to be building a long stream of losing trades. Although I must say my discipline did keep me positive for a few more than just three losses in a row. This was because I had developed the trading system, knew it inside out, and also used a simple money management system I call "SUMM." This money management system will be explained in full in the next chapter.

Now that I'd decided to include seasonal time frames in my systems, I had to be careful not to use just the presence of winners during the same time period as a sorting mechanism. After all, seasonal trading is based on fundamentals such as weather conditions and producer/user demands. I have thoroughly researched the fundamentals behind every one of the trades in this book. The seasonals will work by themselves. By marrying them to *The Mega-Seasonal Trading System,* I have included all of the mechanical system trading necessities: a buy/sell signal, a protective stop and a trailing stop.

As I mentioned, *The Mega-Seasonal Trading System* is basically a simple channel breakout system. For novice traders who may be unfamiliar with the term, a price channel is a band of highs and lows that have been made over a specified period of time. The time length can be anything from minutes to years. It depends upon the time frame of the trader.

The high price channel uses the very highest price the commodity traded at during the time period. The low price channel uses the very lowest price the commodity traded at during the time period. For example let's construct a simple five-day high price channel of the following data:

DATE	HIGH	5-DAY HIGH CHANNEL
11/02/02	123.00	
11/03/02	121.75	
11/04/02	121.00	
11/05/02	122.00	
11/06/02	121.50	123.00 (from 11/02/02)

The highest price for this five-day period is 123.00, made on 11/02/02. Let's move a day forward.

DATE	HIGH	5-DAY HIGH CHANNEL
11/02/02	123.00	
11/03/02	121.75	
11/04/02	121.00	
11/05/02	122.00	
11/06/02	121.50	123.00 (11/02/02 thru 11/06/02)
11/09/02	121.75	122.00 (11/03/02 thru 11/09/02)

Notice there is a new five-day high of 122.00 made on 11/05/02. The old five-day high of 123.00 made on 11/02/02 is no longer in the last five trading days. As each trading day passes you have a different set of data to look over. You lose the oldest day and add the most recent day. Each channel is constructed in the same way as this one, although the number of time periods used differs.

Now, let's turn to the building of a price channel for lows. It's nearly the same as what we've just done, with two differences. First, instead of using the period highs we use the lows. Second, instead of finding the highest of the prices we find the lowest.

This simplicity of design is the foundation for every *Mega-Seasonal* order; the entry price, the protective stop price and the trailing profit stop price. The system can be done with no more than a piece of paper and a pencil. No expensive computer is needed. If you do have a computer with a charting program installed, you most likely will have this technique already built in.

The *Mega-Seasonal* method uses these channels as an activation price for each of the orders. This is called a Channel Breakout System. A breakout is the penetration of the price channel by a certain number of ticks. Thus, if the high price of a channel is 122.00, your order would be to buy today at 122.00 plus the number of ticks in the signal's rules. This is usually one tick. A tick is the minimum price change that the exchange allows for the commodity being traded. Below is a list of the minimum price changes for the commodities traded in this book.

Commodity	Minimum Price Change	Value of Min. Change
Bean Oil	1 cent per hundred pounds	$ 6.00
Live Cattle	2.5 cents per hundred pounds	$10.00
Corn	0.25 cents per bushel	$12.50
Cotton	5 cents per pound	$25.00
Crude Oil	1 cent per barrel	$10.00
Heating Oil	1 cent per 100 gallons	$ 4.20
Lean Hogs	2.5 cents per hundred pounds	$10.00
Kansas City Wheat	0.25 cents per bushel	$12.50
Orange Juice	5 cents per pound	$ 7.50
Pork Bellies	2.5 cents per pound	$10.00
Soybeans	0.25 cents per bushel	$12.50
#11 World Sugar	1 cent per hundred pounds	$11.20
Unleaded Gasoline	1 cent per hundred gallons	$ 4.20

Now that I've explained the channel breakout approach, let's walk through the first example - Corn Trade #1. This trade enters only on the short side of the market. Following along with this example should help clear up any questions you may have about the system.

Rules for Corn Trade #1:

1. Enters short December Corn from the first trading day after May 12th through the first trading day of August. (This is the trade entry window for the trade. Only during this time frame are entry orders active.)

2. Place a short entry stop 1 tick (0.25 cents) below the low of the last 21 trading days. Move the entry stop as the 21-day low changes. (Subtract 1 tick, 0.25 cents, from the lowest price made during the previous 21 trading days. This is today's entry price. As the 21-day low increases, enter new entry stops. Continue this until the order is filled or you are no longer in the entry time window.)

3. Place a protective stop 1 tick (0.25 cents) above the high of the last 2 trading days. (Find the highest price made during the last 2 trading days, not counting the day of entry. Add 1 tick, 0.25 cents, to that price. This is the protective stop for the entry. **Note**: This protective stop **does not change** until it is replaced by the trailing profit stop.)

4. When the high of the last 11 trading days is equal to or less than the entry price, move the stop down to 1 tick (0.25 cents) above the 11-day high. As the 11-day high decreases, this stop price is lowered.

5. If stopped out while still in the trade entry window, go back to #2 and enter new entry orders.

6. Exit this trade on the close of the first trading day after August 6th.

Following is the "Trade Action Diary" for the 2000 Corn Trade #1. As further help, a spreadsheet of the daily high, low, 21-day low channel and 11-day high channel follows the diary. On the page following the spreadsheet is a chart with the two channels marked.

Trade Action Diary - Corn Trade #1 for 2000

DATE   **ACTIONS TAKEN**

05/15/00

(Pre-open)   This is the first trading day after May 12th and the first day to begin entering orders. For entry we use the 21-day price channel of lows. Looking at the daily data for December Corn, you can see that the lowest price for the last 21 days is 248.75 made on 4/11/00. Now you know the entry price. Next, you need to know the protective stop for the trade. Notice Rule #3. The protective stop for this trade is 1 tick (0.25 cents) above the 2-day high. In this case the 2-day high is 264.00 made on 05/12/00. This makes the protective stop 264.25 (264.00 + 0.25). Your risk is the difference between the entry price and the protective stop. (The 264.25 protective stop less the 248.50 (248.75-0.25) entry stop which equals 15.75 cents or $788 per contract.) You need to know the risk so you can decide the number of contracts to trade, if you are going to use the "SUMM" money management system explained in Chapter 3. When you have an active entry order already entered with your broker, and the 2-day high changes, the risk should be recomputed. The number of contracts bought or sold on the order may then need to be changed. To keep things simple we'll trade only one contract in the examples. Now call your broker and enter an order to "Sell 1 December Corn contract at 248.75 (248.50-0.25) stop, GTC." (GTC is trader's talk for "Good 'Til Canceled.") (Optional: If you are lucky enough to have a broker who takes contingency orders, also enter your protective stop order like this - "If the corn order is filled, then Buy 1 December Corn at 264.25 stop, GTC." Remember that as the 2-day high changes, this protective stop order will also need to be changed.)

05/25/00

(Pre-open)   The 21-day low has increased to 249.75. Call your broker and tell him to cancel and replace your original order. The new order is: "Sell 1 December Corn at 249.50 (249.75-0.25) stop GTC." (Now, if you placed a contingency order, this too will have to be changed. The new protective stop price is 260.00 (259.75 made on 5/23 plus 0.25), GTC. Presently the risk on this trade is 14.75 cents or $738 per contract.)

05/25/00   Your broker calls with your fill. You sold 1 December Corn at 249.50. If you were not able to place a contingency protective stop, this is the time to place the protective stop. Tell your broker to "Buy 1 December Corn at 260.00 (the high of 259.75 made on 5/23 plus 0.25 cents) GTC. (If you have placed a contingency protective stop, then your broker will tell you he's already entered that order.)   If at all possible, it's best to place contingency orders. If the protective stop order isn't in, and the broker is unable to contact you, you will be trading without a protective stop. This is something you should never do!

06/14/00

(Pre-open)   You've been tracking the 11-day high. As of yesterday's close the highest high of the 11 past trading days is now 248.75. This price is now below your entry price. The trailing profit stop is now active. You call your broker and cancel and replace the stop order that's on the books. The new order reads "Buy 1 December Corn at 249.00 (248.75+0.25) stop, GTC."

06/20/00

(Pre-open)   The 11-day high has again dropped. Call your broker and cancel and replace your stop order. The new stop price is 247.25. Now things start getting exciting. You're beginning to lock in profits and that's always fun.

06/21/00

(Pre-open)   Another day and another drop in the 11-day high. This time the high is down to 245.00. Things are going well. Call your broker and cancel and replace your stop order. The new stop price is 245.25.

06/22/00

(Pre-open)   The 11-day high has dropped to 242.00. Call your broker and lower your stop price to 242.25. Yesterday December Corn closed at 223.75. You have a paper profit of 25.75 cents per bushel or $1,288 per contract. Pay as little attention as you can to this number. If you must watch your paper profit, use the profit stop number and not the close. The more attention you give to the day-by-day profit number, the more you'll be tempted

18

to bail out of the trade. This is the action many beginning traders choose. As they continue to trade this way, the size of the profit at which they will exit the trade becomes smaller and smaller. Eventually they take any profit that they can, while still taking the same risk. The final outcome of this style of trading is a risk-reward ratio of less than 1 to 1 and an account balance of $0.

06/23/00

(Pre-open)   The 11-day high is continuing to decline. Call your broker and cancel and replace the trailing stop, moving the price down to 241.00 (240.75+0.25).

06/27/00

(Pre-open)   The 11-day high has dropped 8.75 cents to 232.00. Call your broker and lower your stop price again. The new stop is 232.25.

06/28/00

(Pre-open)   Another new lower high channel. Call your broker and lower the trailing stop price to 230.50.

06/29/00

(Pre-open)   Call your broker. The 11-day high has dropped to 230.00 making the new stop 230.25.

07/05/00

(Pre-open)   The 11-day high has dropped to 226.50. Call your broker and lower your stop again.

07/11/00

(Pre-open)   The 11-day high has dropped to 222.00. Call your broker and lower your stop.

07/12/00

(Pre-open)   Another new 11-day high and another call to your broker to lower the trailing profit stop to 218.25 (218.00+0.25).

07/14/00

(Pre-open)   The 11-day high has dropped to 217.00 and the new stop is 217.25.

07/18/00

(Pre-open)   Call your broker. There's a new stop number. This time your stop is 216.75.

07/19/00

(Pre-open)   The 11-day high has dropped to 206.25 and your new stop is 206.50.

07/25/00

(Pre-open)   Another big break in the 11-day high. The new high is 201.25 and the stop is 201.50.

08/07/00

(Pre-open)   This is the first trading day after August 6th - the exit day. You call your broker and place an order to Buy 1 December Corn on the close. You must keep the trailing profit stop at 201.25 active. If your broker allows, tell him that one order cancels the other.

08/07/00

(After close) Your broker calls to tell you your stop order has been filled on the close at 190.00. If you were not able to enter the "one order cancels the other order," you must cancel the order to Buy 1 December Corn at 212.25 stop GTC. You just made $2,975 profit.

DECEMBER 2000 CORN

DATE	HIGH	LOW	21-DAY LOW	11-DAY HIGH
03/01/00	250.25	248.00		
03/02/00	249.75	247.25		
03/03/00	250.75	249.00		
03/06/00	253.25	249.50		
03/07/00	253.50	249.00		
03/08/00	252.25	248.50		
03/09/00	254.00	252.25		
03/10/00	253.25	250.75		
03/13/00	257.00	253.50		
03/14/00	262.00	256.50		
03/15/00	262.25	259.50		
03/16/00	262.50	257.75		
03/17/00	264.25	261.25		
03/20/00	260.25	256.50		
03/21/00	260.00	255.50		
03/22/00	259.00	256.00		
03/23/00	257.25	254.50		
03/24/00	258.75	256.00		
03/27/00	259.25	255.75		
03/28/00	257.00	251.00		
03/29/00	253.25	250.00	247.25	
03/30/00	258.25	254.50	247.25	
03/31/00	262.00	259.00	248.50	
04/03/00	264.25	259.25	248.50	
04/04/00	259.50	255.50	248.50	
04/05/00	259.75	256.00	248.50	
04/06/00	255.75	252.50	250.00	
04/07/00	255.25	251.25	250.00	
04/10/00	253.25	251.00	250.00	
04/11/00	252.75	248.75	248.75	
04/12/00	252.00	249.50	248.75	
04/13/00	254.50	251.50	248.75	
04/18/00	252.25	250.00	248.75	
04/19/00	255.00	250.50	248.75	
04/20/00	254.50	250.25	248.75	
04/24/00	255.00	251.75	248.75	
04/25/00	257.75	255.00	248.75	
04/26/00	258.75	254.00	248.75	

22

DATE	HIGH	LOW	21-DAY LOW	11-DAY HIGH
04/27/00	253.50	251.50	248.75	
04/28/00	252.75	249.75	248.75	
05/01/00	262.00	254.50	248.75	
05/02/00	265.50	261.75	248.75	
05/03/00	273.50	265.00	248.75	
05/04/00	267.75	264.50	248.75	
05/05/00	265.50	261.75	248.75	
05/08/00	262.00	257.00	248.75	
05/09/00	256.75	254.50	248.75	
05/10/00	262.50	257.00	248.75	
05/11/00	262.75	258.75	248.75	
05/12/00	**264.00**	257.50	**248.75**	
05/15/00	258.50	252.00	249.50	
05/16/00	258.25	252.75	249.75	
05/17/00	255.00	250.25	249.75	
05/18/00	260.25	255.25	249.75	
05/19/00	259.50	255.75	249.75	
05/22/00	262.00	256.25	249.75	
05/23/00	259.75	256.50	249.75	
05/24/00	255.25	252.25	**249.75**	
05/25/00	254.25	247.75	247.75	264.00
05/26/00	252.50	249.00	247.75	264.00
05/30/00	245.50	241.50	241.50	262.00
05/31/00	245.00	241.25	241.25	262.00
06/01/00	247.50	243.25	241.25	262.00
06/02/00	248.75	244.00	241.25	262.00
06/05/00	247.00	242.75	241.25	262.00
06/06/00	245.00	241.75	241.25	262.00
06/07/00	242.00	238.25	238.25	259.75
06/08/00	239.50	236.50	236.50	255.25
06/09/00	240.75	238.00	236.50	254.25
06/12/00	232.00	228.00	228.00	252.50
06/13/00	230.25	227.50	227.50	**248.75**
06/14/00	225.50	220.50	220.50	248.75
06/15/00	227.25	224.00	220.50	248.75
06/16/00	230.00	227.25	220.50	248.75
06/19/00	225.50	223.50	220.50	**247.00**
06/20/00	223.75	220.75	220.50	**245.00**
06/21/00	225.50	221.75	220.50	**242.00**
06/22/00	226.50	223.00	220.50	**240.75**
06/23/00	222.00	219.00	219.00	240.75

DATE	HIGH	LOW	21-DAY LOW	11-DAY HIGH
06/26/00	216.25	213.75	213.75	**232.00**
06/27/00	218.00	216.00	213.75	**230.25**
06/28/00	216.00	212.75	212.75	**230.00**
06/29/00	217.00	213.00	212.75	230.00
06/30/00	216.50	205.00	205.00	230.00
07/03/00	204.50	199.25	199.25	**226.50**
07/05/00	204.75	201.00	199.25	226.50
07/06/00	202.75	199.25	199.25	226.50
07/07/00	206.25	201.50	199.25	226.50
07/10/00	199.00	196.00	196.00	**222.00**
07/11/00	199.75	196.50	196.00	**218.00**
07/12/00	198.00	192.00	192.00	218.00
07/13/00	199.25	196.25	192.00	**217.00**
07/14/00	196.50	193.00	192.00	217.00
07/17/00	192.50	190.00	190.00	**216.50**
07/18/00	195.75	192.25	190.00	**206.25**
07/19/00	195.00	190.50	190.00	206.25
07/20/00	199.00	193.00	190.00	206.25
07/21/00	200.00	197.25	190.00	206.25
07/24/00	201.25	195.50	190.00	**201.25**
07/25/00	195.25	193.00	190.00	201.25
07/26/00	194.00	191.25	190.00	201.25
07/27/00	194.75	192.25	190.00	201.25
07/28/00	194.50	191.75	190.00	201.25
07/31/00	194.00	189.25	189.25	201.25
08/01/00	193.75	191.00	189.25	201.25
08/02/00	194.25	192.50	189.25	201.25
08/03/00	194.50	190.50	189.25	201.25
08/04/00	192.75	190.50	189.25	201.25
08/07/00	191.75	189.50	189.25	201.25

DECEMBER 00 CORN

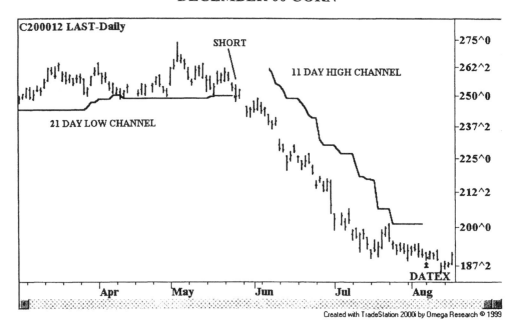

I hope this example helps to explain the simple Mega-Seasonal Breakout System I use to enter and exit trades. Not all the trades in this book are quite as simple as the Corn Trade #1 I've just explained. Some of the trades enter on both sides of the market. The entry system is not that much harder, and in many instances, these double trades are the most profitable. Follow me through the Soybean Oil Trade #1 that follows, and you'll see that it's not much harder than the Corn Trade.

Rules for Soybean Oil Trade #1

1. Enters long or short September Soybean Oil from the first trading day after May 21st through the last trading day of July.

2. Place a long entry stop 1 tick (0.01 cents) above the high of the last 18 trading days **and** place a short entry stop 1 tick (0.01 cents) below the low of the last 18 trading days. Move these entry stops as the 18-day high and 18-day low change.

3. When filled:

   On long: Place a protective stop 1 tick (0.01 cents) under the low of the last 4 trading days. **Note:** This protective stop **does not change** until it is replaced by the trailing profit stop or a reverse entry stop.

   On short: Place a protective stop 1 tick (0.01 cents) above the high of the last 4 trading days. **Note:** This protective stop **does not change** until it is replaced by the trailing profit or a reverse entry stop.

Remember to continue entering the opposite entry orders as described in #2 until you are no longer in the trade entry window. Should you have already entered a long trade via #2 and the short entry price is greater than either the protective stop or the profit stop, replace the protective stop price or profit stop price with the short entry price, thus exiting the current long trade and entering a new short trade. Should you have already entered a short trade via #2 and the long entry price is less than either the protective stop or the profit stop, replace the protective stop price or the profit stop price with the long entry price, thus exiting the current short trade and entering a new long trade.

26

4. If long: When the low of the last 14 trading days is equal to or greater than the entry price, move the stop up to 1 tick (0.01 cents) below the 14-day low. As the 14-day low increases, this stop price is raised.

    If short: When the high of the last 14 trading days is equal to or less than the entry price, move the stop down to 1 tick (0.01 cents) above the 14-day high. As the 14-day high decreases, this stop price is lowered.

5. If stopped out while still in the trade entry window, go back to #2 and enter new entry orders.

6. Exit this trade on the close of the first trading day after August 12th.

Trade Action Diary - Soybean Oil Trade #1 for 2001

DATE	ACTIONS TAKEN

05/22/02

(Pre-open)

This is the first day of the entry window for Soybean Oil Trade #1. Referring to the trade data section that follows, look up the 18-day high and 18-day low (1780 and 1638 respectively). These are the high and low entry channels for the trade. Before entering the orders you must add one tick to the high (1780+1 = 1781) and subtract one tick from the low (1638-1 = 1637). These are the entry stop order prices for today. Next, you should compute the protective stop price for each side of the trade. For the long entry the protective stop is 1709. This is computed by taking the 4-day low of 1710 made on 05/16/02 and subtracting 1 tick or 1 point. The protective stop for the short position is computed by adding 1 tick or 1 point to the 4-day high of 1780 made on 05/21/01. This makes the protective stop for the short trade 1781. Then you should compute the risk for each side of the trade. This will let you know the number of contracts you can trade on each side, considering the amount of risk you are willing to assume. (Note: The risks may be different, and so may the number of contracts you will be able to safely buy or sell.) The long trade risk is the entry stop price of 1781 less the long protective stop price of 1709, or 72 points times $6.00 = $432 per contract. The risk on the short trade is computed in the same way – the 1781 protective stop less the 1637 entry price, or 144 points times $6.00 = $864 per contract. As in the previous example, this example will trade only 1 contract on each side.

Now it's time to call your broker. Tell him you want to "Buy 1 September Soybean Oil at 1781 stop, GTC and Sell 1 September Soybean Oil at 1637 stop GTC." If your broker allows contingency orders you should put in the protective stop orders also. Tell him "If filled on the long order, I'd like to Sell 1 September Soybean Oil at 1709 stop, GTC. And, if filled on the short order, I'd like to Buy 1 September Soybean Oil at 1781 stop, GTC." If you are able to enter contingency orders, remember to call your broker and change the stop prices as the 4-day high and low changes, and your entry orders are still active.

05/22/02

(After-open)   Your broker calls with your fill on the long entry. You bought 1 September Soybean Oil at 1788. (You were filled on the opening at 7 ticks above your stop price. This is called "slippage" in the commodity trading business, and is quite normal.) If you were not able to place a contingency protective stop order, now is the time to place your protective stop for this trade. Tell your broker to "Sell 1 September Soybean Oil at 1709."

06/04/02

(Pre-open)   The 18-day low has risen to 1670. Your new sell price for the short side of this trade is 1669 (the 1670 new 18-day low less 1). Call your broker and cancel and replace your sell order. You have two sell orders on the books, one to exit your long position and one to position yourself on the short side.

06/05/02

(Pre-open)   The 18-day low has risen. Raise your short entry price to 1682.

06/12/02

(Pre-open)   There is a new 18-day low. Call your broker and cancel and replace your short entry order to 1709. Notice that this is the same price as the protective stop order for your long trade. Now you have two orders at this price. Should the price be hit, your long order will be stopped out and your new short order will be filled.

06/13/02

(Pre-open)   The 18-day low has risen again. Call your broker and cancel and replace both your short order and your long protective stop order. The new price for both orders is 1716. Remember that the entry prices are exactly that, entry prices. If one is hit, you must have a position in the direction of the order hit. At times such as this, it will mean that you exit the reverse position in order to enter the new trade.

06/14/02

(Pre-open)   The 18-day low is now 1744. Again, call your broker and cancel and replace both your open orders.

06/15/02

(Pre-open)   The 18-day low has changed again. Change both open orders to the new price of 1754.

06/18/02

(Pre-open)   The 18-day low has risen. Call your broker and cancel and replace both of your sell orders to the new price of 1777.

06/19/02

(Pre-open)   Another new 18-day low, and it's time to call your broker and lower your stop price and short entry price to 1779.

07/11/02

(Pre-open)   The 18-day low has risen. It's time to raise your short entry stop and protective stop price to 1785.

07/25/02

(Pre-open)   Finally, the 14-day low channel has risen to above the entry price of 1788. You call your broker and raise the trailing stop on your long trade to 1811.

07/26/02

(Pre-open)   The 14-day low has increased to 1828. Cancel and replace your long trailing stop. The new price is 1827.

07/29/00

(Pre-open)   The 14-day low continues to rise, locking in your profits. The new trailing stop price is 1864.

07/31/02

(Pre-open)   The 18-day channel of lows has risen to a new high of 1812. You call your broker and raise the short entry price to 1811.

08/01/02

(Pre-open)   Two important things have happened. The first is that we are no longer in the entry time window. The entry order for the short side must be canceled. Secondly, the 14-day low channel has risen and the trailing profit stop must be raised to 1893.

08/02/02

(Pre-open)   Again, the 14-day low has risen. Cancel and replace your long trailing stop price to 1913.

08/13/02

(Pre-open)   Today is the day. You call your broker and tell him to enter an order to "Sell 1 September Soybean Oil on the close." If your broker will take it, tie this order to the trailing stop by making one order cancel the other. There is always a chance that both orders could get hit during the close and you would end up short 1 contract. If your broker will not accept this kind of order, it would be a good idea for you to check the price September Soybean Oil is trading at a few minutes before the close. Should the most recent price be quite a distance from the trailing stop price, which is usually the case, call your broker and cancel the trailing stop order.

08/13/02

(After-close) You broker calls you with the fill. You sold your September Soybean Oil at 2062 for a profit of $1644.

Hopefully, these two examples have served to make my Mega-Seasonal Trading System easy and understandable. It's not that hard, just very simple math.

SEPTEMBER 2002 SOYBEAN OIL

DATE	HIGH	LOW	18-DAY HIGH	18-DAY LOW	14-DAY LOW
03/01/02	1652	1608			
03/04/02	1658	1633			
03/05/02	1673	1643			
03/06/02	1662	1653			
03/07/02	1695	1672			
03/08/02	1704	1680			
03/11/02	1700	1675			
03/12/02	1715	1692			
03/13/02	1711	1690			
03/14/02	1735	1707			
03/15/02	1756	1735			
03/18/02	1742	1693			
03/19/02	1697	1675			
03/20/02	1696	1660			
03/21/02	1672	1570			
03/22/02	1673	1658			
03/25/02	1660	1642			
03/26/02	1653	1643	1756	1570	
03/27/02	1661	1652	1756	1570	
03/28/02	1695	1678	1756	1570	
04/01/02	1721	1697	1756	1570	
04/02/02	1720	1692	1756	1570	
04/03/02	1697	1674	1756	1570	
04/04/02	1688	1671	1756	1570	
04/05/02	1721	1695	1756	1570	
04/08/02	1722	1691	1756	1570	
04/09/02	1703	1686	1756	1570	
04/10/02	1710	1695	1756	1570	
04/11/02	1706	1697	1742	1570	
04/12/02	1713	1693	1722	1570	
04/15/02	1725	1685	1725	1570	
04/16/02	1703	1678	1725	1570	
04/17/02	1735	1708	1735	1642	
04/18/02	1745	1718	1745	1642	
04/19/02	1742	1733	1745	1643	
04/22/02	1775	1742	1775	1652	
04/23/02	1742	1730	1775	1671	
04/24/02	1752	1741	1775	1671	

DATE	HIGH	LOW	18-DAY HIGH	18-DAY LOW	14-DAY LOW
04/25/02	1744	1711	1775	1671	
04/29/02	1694	1660	1775	1660	
04/30/02	1680	1653	1775	1653	
05/01/02	1662	1647	1775	1647	
05/02/02	1676	1663	1775	1647	
05/03/02	1663	1649	1775	1647	
05/06/02	1654	1639	1775	1639	
05/07/02	1667	1638	1775	1638	
05/08/02	1688	1670	1775	1638	
05/09/02	1714	1689	1775	1638	
05/10/02	1738	1698	1775	1638	
05/13/02	1724	1705	1775	1638	
05/14/02	1705	1693	1775	1638	
05/15/02	1705	1683	1775	1638	
05/16/02	1740	(1710)	1775	1638	
05/17/02	1731	1717	**1752**	1638	
05/20/02	1775	1744	**1775**	1638	
05/21/02	(1780)	1755	(1780)	(1638)	
05/22/02	1812	1778	1812	1638	1638
05/23/02	1814	1780		1638	1638
05/24/02	1802	1788		1638	1638
05/28/02	1847	1806		1638	**1670**
05/29/02	1846	1822		1638	**1683**
05/30/02	1834	1817		1638	1683
05/31/02	1890	1845		1638	1683
06/03/02	1884	1860		**1670**	1683
06/04/02	1908	1874		**1683**	1683
06/05/02	1899	1879		1683	**1710**
06/06/02	1911	1892		1683	**1717**
06/07/02	1876	1852		1683	**1744**
06/10/02	1828	1807		1683	**1755**
06/11/02	1835	1812		**1710**	**1778**
06/12/02	1823	1791		**1717**	**1780**
06/13/02	1812	1780		**1744**	1780
06/14/02	1843	1816		**1755**	1780
06/17/02	1843	1819		**1778**	1780
06/18/02	1817	1805		**1780**	1780
06/19/02	1815	1786		1780	1780
06/20/02	1801	1788		1780	1780
06/21/02	1823	1788		1780	1780
06/24/02	1840	1820		1780	1780

DATE	HIGH	LOW	18-DAY HIGH	18-DAY LOW	14-DAY LOW
06/25/02	1833	1810		1780	1780
06/26/02	1828	1798		1780	1780
06/27/02	1837	1819		1780	1780
06/28/02	1868	1845		1780	1780
07/01/02	1875	1852		1780	1780
07/02/02	1862	1813		1780	1780
07/03/02	1842	1786		1780	**1786**
07/05/02	1841	1812		1780	1786
07/08/02	1880	1828		1780	1786
07/09/02	1900	1870		1780	1786
07/10/02	1890	1872		**1786**	1786
07/11/02	1898	1865		1786	1786
07/12/02	1940	1894		1786	1786
07/15/02	2013	1978		1786	1786
07/16/02	1997	1961		1786	1786
07/17/02	1990	1961		1786	1786
07/18/02	1995	1953		1786	1786
07/19/02	2008	1965		1786	1786
07/22/02	2035	2015		1786	1786
07/23/02	2003	1955		1786	1786
07/24/02	1999	1965		1786	**1812**
07/25/02	1963	1936		1786	**1828**
07/26/02	1984	1943		1786	**1865**
07/29/02	1940	1914		1786	1865
07/30/02	1978	1935		**1812**	1865
07/31/02	2051	2015			**1894**
08/01/02	2070	2004			**1914**
08/02/02	2043	2018			1914
08/05/02	2002	1980			1914
08/06/02	2017	1990			1914
08/07/02	2023	1992			1914
08/08/02	2013	1998			1914
08/09/02	2005	1980			1914
08/12/02	2090	2053			1914

SEPTEMBER 02 SOYBEAN OIL

BO200209 LAST-Daily

18 Day High Channel

LONG

18 Day Low Channel

14 Day Low Channel

Date X

Created with TradeStation 2000i by Omega Research ® 1999

- Chapter 3 -

THE "SUMM" SYSTEM OF MONEY MANAGEMENT

This may be a bit of a surprise to hear, but a good trading system will not necessarily make you a good or even profitable trader. You see, even the best trading system in the world can produce losses. And if you do not have a good sound system of money management, these losses will cause you to quit trading before you give the system a fair chance to make a profit.

What is money management? Simply stated, money management is a mathematical system for deciding how much of your total trading account to risk on each trade. This risk is based upon simple statistics and account size, not on any market factors. Money management is not a method for setting stop loss orders, although stop loss orders figure into the formula for calculating the initial per contract risk. The risk on a trade is simply the entry price less the protective stop price times the dollar value per point. Using this dollar risk per contract, you can then decide the number of contracts to safely trade for the size of your trading account.

Remember, trading is a business, very much like any other business. Many businesses fail, and certainly the business of commodity trading has both successes and failures. The main reason behind any business' failure is under-capitalization. In other words, the business runs out of expense money before it can become profitable. This is just as true in the trading business as it is in any other business.

In the trading business the only real expense is a losing trade. Even the best trading system will have bad runs and suffer a series of losses before hitting winners. This is where a good money management system becomes necessary.

The money management system must be founded on rules that will keep the "trading business" in the black with enough money to assure that there is always sufficient capital to take the next trade and the next trade and the next.

This isn't as easy as it sounds. Fortunately, many very learned people have spent unknown numbers of hours working on the solution to this problem. Much of this work was done in relation to the gambling business, and not trading. Yet, it so happens that there are quite a few similarities between gambling and trading, so this research is viable and usable for the futures trader.

There are two well known methods of money management in the gambling world, the Martingale and the Anti-Martingale systems. Both systems assume that the probability of winning the bet is 50%, and that a winning bet is paid off at even money. Although this is not identical to normal commodity trading, it is a safe way to research money management.

The "Martingale" system has a standard bet size that is continuously doubled after a loss. The first bet might be $1. If this bet were lost, the next bet would be $2. And if this bet also lost, the next bet would be $4. This doubling continues until there is a winning bet. After a win the bet returns to $1 and begins doubling again.

This system actually works, in theory. However, there are two problems. The first is that the player must have an unlimited bankroll that will allow him to keep doubling the bet until he finally has a winner. In the above example, should the player suffer 6 losses in a row, the 7th bet would be for $32. And the chance for 6 losses in a row is a definite possibility. If the player were to make 100 bets, he would experience a series of six losses at least once or possibly twice. After the win, the bankroll will have grown by only the size of the original bet, $1. All the rest of the winnings will pay back for previous losses in the string. Thus, eventually, he will be risking a lot on a bet ($32) which, should he win, will yield only the minimum bet ($1) in total profit.

The second problem with the "Martingale" system is that the gambler will need to find an opponent who will allow unlimited sized bets. This, of course, is where the whole system falls apart. Making the logical assumption that the "casino" understands the "Martingale" betting system, the maximum size of a single bet is limited. Thus the number of times a bet may be doubled is limited. This cuts the system off at the knees, often leaving the gambler with a string of losses and no eventual maximum win.

The second system is the "Anti-Martingale" betting system. As the name suggests, it is the reverse of the "Martingale" system. The "Anti-Martingale" methodology is to double the size of the bet after a win and continue the doubling until a loss. This has the same bet size limit problem as the "Martingale" system. However, unlike the Martingale system, which at least worked in theory, this system has one more problem. The last bet is always a loser! Since the size of this last bet is the total amount of all previous money won plus one standard bet, you will be guaranteed a loss unless you use a predetermined number of wins to stop the doubling of the bet and then begin again with the minimum bet.

These two money management systems have spawned quite a few variations – Fixed Fractional, Percent Risk, Percent Volatility, Optimal f, Secure f, Asymmetrical Leverage and the Kelly Strategy. Most of these variations have one thing in common – they're fairly complex. They are designed by professors of mathematics who claim that their ideas will produce the greatest returns. Their theories are backed up by pages and pages of confusing formulas containing strings of Greek letters. Unfortunately, these ideas are just theories, and those building them are not experienced futures traders. All of these systems have supporters who have investigated their value and believe in their individual importance. I'm sure that each system has some value, but I like to keep it simple and go with the one money management method which I know other winning traders use successfully, the Fixed Risk Strategy.

The Fixed Risk Strategy is a simple money management method. It limits the risk on each trade to a percentage of the total trading account. That's all there is to it. This simple strategy automatically increases the size of the dollar risk when winning, and decreases the dollar risk when losing. This is done in the most logical of ways. The percent of risk does not change, but the size of the account does, thereby increasing the dollar risk. Let's take a look at the simple math of the basic underlying equation.

First, we need to know the probability of a successful trade. The trades in this book all have a historical 70% or greater chance of earning a profit. Another way of saying this is that the average trade has a 30% chance of producing a loss. We look at the percentage of producing a loser because what we are attempting to figure out is the "Risk of Ruin."

Now, let's look at the "Risk of Ruin" chart on the next page. The left side column lists the number of losses in a row. The middle column lists the number of times this number of losses will happen in 100 trades (I'll explain why this column is included later in this chapter). The right column lists the number of times the number of losses will happen in 1000 trades. This is the most important column. I want to remain in this business a long time. If I take all the trades in this book each year for 30 to 40 years, I will make about 1000 trades.

30% PROBABILITY OF LOSS		
Number of Losses in a Row	**Times in 100**	**Times in 1000**
1	30	300
2	9	90
3	2.7	27
4	0.81	8.1
5	0.243	2.43
6	0.0729	0.729
7	0.02187	0.2187
8	0.006561	0.06561
9	0.0019683	0.019683
10	0.00059049	0.0059049

Looking at the column for 1000 trades, I search for the first number that is under 1. That row is 6 losses. Being less than the number 1, the statistics say that during my trading career of 1000 trades, I would probably never suffer 6 losses in a row. Also notice, though, that this chance is 0.729. This is quite near the magic number 1 that would put me out of business. To be safe, I would expect that I just might have 6 losses in a row and would concentrate on 7 losses for my mathematics.

Knowing that 7 losses in a row is the greatest number of losses I can expect, I then have to figure what percentage of my total account I am willing to lose before I make the decision that my trading system is no longer performing as expected. Most professional traders use the 50% level. Should my account drop by half (50%), it's time to call it quits.

The rest of the math is simple. If the most of my account I'm willing to lose is 50%, and the greatest number of losses in a row is 7, then the largest risk for each of the 7 trades is 50% divided by 7, or 7%. This 7% risk of your total trading account should be the maximum per trade risk you take.

Now, to double-check these figures against actual trading results, I went through the nearly one thousand trades made from 1973 through 2002 listed in this book. What was the worst string of losses? Six. The math was close, but not perfect, so my conservative bent to use 7 losses and not 6 proved correct. In fact, during the 30 years of history I checked, a series of six losses happened only a few times.

Had I been risking only 7% of my account, and each of the six losses been for the total 7%, I would have lost only 42% of my account. I would have still been above the magic 50% figure. This would give me one more shot at a winning trade.

Even though the 7% risk proved itself out, I am still too conservative to come this close to going out of the trading business. One way to take another statistical look at this is to change the assumption of 70% winning trades to a much lower 50%. This would make the chance of a loss also 50%. Take a look at the following chart which incorporates this assumption of a reduced winning percentage.

50% PROBABILITY OF LOSS

Number of Losses in a Row	Times in 100	Times in 1000
1	50	500
2	25	250
3	12.5	125
4	6.25	62.5
5	3.125	31.25
6	1.5625	15.625
7	0.78125	7.8125
8	0.390625	3.90625
9	0.1953125	1.953125
10	0.09765625	0.9765625
11	0.048828125	0.48828125
12	0.0244140625	0.244140625
13	0.0122070313	0.1220703125
14	0.0061035156	0.0610351563
15	0.0030517578	0.0305175781

Using the same method as was used with the 70% profitability study, I look down "Times in 1000" column on the 50% Loss Spreadsheet until I find the first number under one. There it is, on the line with "10 losses in a row." This works out perfectly. If I assume that I will not have to suffer from more than 10 losses in a row, and I prefer to risk only 50% of my trading account, the amount of the maximum risk per trade is 5%. This falls perfectly in line with what most professional commodity money managers suggest. It is widely known in the industry that using greater than 5% is considered "gun-slinging" and that many of the pros use far less.

For quick and easy reference, I've chosen to nickname this money management system "SUMM" (Simple Uncomplicated Money Management).

You will notice that "SUMM" is mentioned in the Performance History for each of the seasonal trades. This will allow those of you who choose to use the "SUMM" money management system to estimate the yearly gross profit you can expect for the trade, assuming all goes perfectly. The "Yearly Percentage Equity Growth Chart" that follows below details the historical returns for the last 30 years on a trading account using the "SUMM" method. These figures were computed using a personalized mathematical formula, and therefore could not be exactly replicated by any account. There are times that fractions of a contract would have been traded, which is not possible in actual trading. Following the "Yearly Percentage Equity Growth Chart" is a chart of the combined historical equity growth of the account. As you can see by these results, the trades in this book have performed superbly!

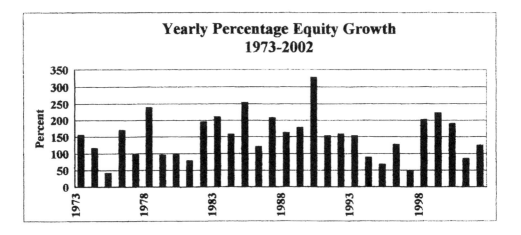

This chart shows the amazing yearly profitability of the trades in this book. I'd like to point out that 70% of the years produced greater than 100% account equity growth. Only 2 out of the 30 years showed less than 50% growth, one 34% and the other 41%. Also note that there were no losing years!

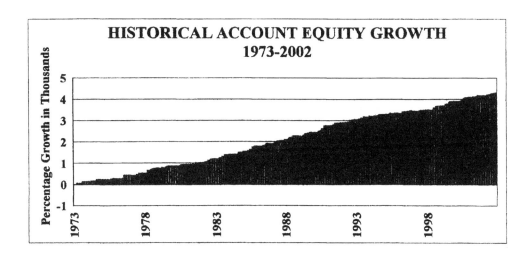

One common question naturally arises: "Can this SUMM system be used with a small trading account?" Yes, it can. In fact, money management is more important for the small trader/novice trader than the larger professional trader. As he is new to the business, the novice trader is far more likely to make simple mistakes and often is trading simply as a sideline.

Yet, what if the 5% per position risk on your trading account turns out to be too small to take trades? Well, addressing that question, I'd like to first point out that one of the major filters I used on all the trades in this book was the initial risk. As mentioned previously, this was an idea suggested to me by readers of my last book. So, unless you have a particularly small trading account, you should be able to take some of the trades in this book. Especially watch the corn, soybean oil, crude oil (there's a mini-contract of 400 bbls traded), orange juice and world sugar trades. As I write this, I'm sitting on a long trade in world sugar that had an initial risk of only $250 plus commission. This means that an account in the $5,000 to $6,000 range would have been able to take this trade. Just to let you know how profitable these trades can be, this sugar trade has so far earned a paper profit of $1,982 per contract.

Now, if you feel that you still are unable to take the trades you want, you have a decision to make. There are a couple of ways to go. If you're very conservative you might do best by just paper trading these trades and saving trading capital. This may prove boring, but will give you some experience in computing the entry, stop and profit stop figures.

If, on the other hand, you're more of a risk taker, you can increase the size of the risk on each trade and/or increase the percentage amount of your total account you are willing to lose. That's why I included a column entitled "Times in 100" on the "50% Loss Chart."

Look down that column. When you get to 7 losses in a row, the "Times in 100" falls below the magic figure of one. This means that, statistically, if you trade 100 times you should not suffer 7 losses in a row. However, statistics are one thing and reality is another. You are taking a greater risk assuming you will never suffer 7 losses in a row.

Once you've established the 7 loss limit you must look at the size of your account. If we assume that you are willing to risk only 50% of your total account, then your risk limitation is 7% (50% / 7 = 7%). Is this enough to take most of the trades in this book? Yes, if your account is around $12,000 - $15,000. Yet, if you are willing to risk your entire account, which would yield a risk of 14%, then you would need an account of only $7,200! This is a genuinely risky strategy, but at least statistically it should work. If you do choose to utilize this high risk money management strategy, be sure to lessen the percentage risk quickly as profits (hopefully) begin to pile up. Your goal here is to grow your account to the size where you can trade with only a 5% risk.

- Chapter 4 -

SOYBEAN OIL

Product Information: *(A brief narrative on the commodity.)*

Soybean Oil is one of the two main products of the soybean plant. The other main product being soybean meal. Both products are particularly healthy for human consumption. Due to these health benefits, half of the soybean oil produced in the United States goes into the manufacture of shortening and margarine, replacing higher fat foods.

Market Information: *(Futures contract information.)*

Soybean Oil has been traded on the Chicago Board of Trade since 1950. The size of a Soybean Oil contract is 60,000 lbs. The trading symbol is "BO" for bean oil. The contract months traded are January, March, May, July, August, September, October and December. The Chicago Board of Trade also trades options on these futures contracts.

Demand Information: *(A discussion of the demand side of the supply/demand equation.)*

The demand for Soybean Oil continues to grow as new uses are discovered and additional health benefits are announced. Price seems to be of little consequence to demand. This is due to the fact that the actual cost of the Soybean Oil is only a small part of the eventual price of the products in which it's used. The United States is the largest producer of Soybean Oil, followed by Brazil.

Supply Information: *(A discussion of the supply side of the supply/demand equation.)*

The supply of Soybean Oil is dependent upon the supply of soybeans. The weather in the United States Midwest and Brazil are all important factors. (For further explanation, see Chapter 14 on Soybeans.)

Reports: *(Important reports that affect the price of the commodity.)*

Crop Production

Crop Progress

Export Sales

Grain Stocks

Supply & Demand Estimate

Prospective Plantings

SOYBEAN OIL TRADE #1

Fundamental Commentary: *(A condensed discussion of the trade's fundamentals.)*

Soybean Oil is one of the two major products of the soybean. As soybean prices are buffeted by the prevailing weather conditions during the planting and growing stages, so are the prices of the products. Soybean Oil Trade #1 positions an envelope of entry stops around the price congestion that normally develops during this time frame. Once the breakout comes, Soybean Oil Trade #1 will jump on board the trend and start piling up profits.

Performance History

1960-2002

Total Years Examined *(Years over which research was performed.)* 43

Profitable Years *(Seasonal years, not individual trades.)* 34   (81%)

Losing Years *(Seasonal years, not individual trades.)* 9   (19%)

Inactive Years *(Years in which entry orders were not activated.)* 0

1973-2002

(In 1973, the commodity markets changed - higher volatility, greater speculative interest. If all data were used, 1960-2002, the following numbers would have been dangerously skewed and virtually useless. These figures are of great importance and must be as accurate as possible.)

Total Net Profit $55,986

(Gross profit less gross loss, commissions and slippage are not deducted.)

50

Average Profit $2,383
(Again, this is not individual trades, but the average profit per profitable seasonal year.)

Average Loss $716
(Not individual trades, but the average loss per losing year.)

Profit-to-Loss Ratio 3.33
(Average Profit divided by Average Loss. Ideally this should be around 3 to 1. Unfortunately, this is very hard to achieve. A 2 to 1 ratio is good.)

Total Profits/Total Losses 16.63
(Total yearly profits divided by total yearly losses. In other words, dollars won versus dollars lost.)

Average Yearly "SUMM" Percent Profit 12.3%
(Yearly percentage growth in total account size using the "SUMM" money management system.)

Home Run Percentage 36.7%
(A home run is a seasonal that increases your total account by 15% or more.)

Performance Commentary: *(Important points to note on the figures contained in the performance history report.)*

   This is a great trade. The high percentage of profitable trades spread over 43 years, with an excellent profit-to-loss ratio and a home run expectation of better than 1 in every 3 years, makes this an excellent trade for every size account.

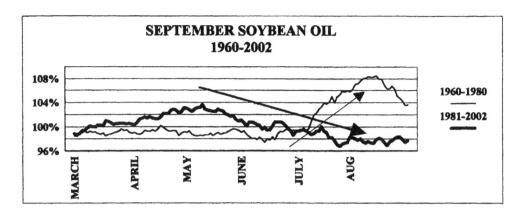

SEPTEMBER SOYBEAN OIL
1960-2002

1960-1980

1981-2002

CHART COMMENTS:

Set-Up: *(A discussion of the most likely chart set-up for a profitable trade.)*

September Bean Oil normally rallies into March - April. At times the rally may last as long as mid-May. Then the market goes through a slow but steady decline, forming a multi-month consolidation range. This formation is roughly the same whether the eventual outcome is bullish or bearish. Should prices break through on the upside, Bean Oil Trade #1 will enter the long side. Should prices fall, you'll be in on the price decline.

After Entry: *(What's most likely to happen after entry.)*

Long trades experience a quick and powerful up move. These often begin just after the Fourth of July.

Short trades tend to meander down slowly, creating short-term price consolidation ranges before breaking out to the downside.

Topping: *(A description of the most likely topping action for long trades.)*

Often this rally ends with the same violent action as it experienced on the way up. Prices move up one day and down the next. Limit days are not unusual. This haphazard movement eventually creates a wide consolidation top (normally during the month of August).

Bottoming: *(A description of the most likely bottoming action for short trades.)*

If the market is moving down, expect a price consolidation range during August. This range is normally much narrower than the topping consolidation range discussed above.

Rules for Soybean Oil Trade #1

1. Enters long or short September Soybean Oil from the first trading day after May 21st through the last trading day of July.

2. Place a long entry stop 1 tick (0.01 cents) above the high of the last 18 trading days **and** place a short entry stop 1 tick (0.01 cents) below the low of the last 18 trading days. Move these entry stops as the 18-day high and 18-day low change.

3. When filled:

   On long: Place a protective stop 1 tick (0.01 cents) under the low of the last 4 trading days. **Note**: This protective stop **does not change** until it is replaced by the trailing profit stop or a reverse entry stop.

   On short: Place a protective stop 1 tick (0.01 cents) above the high of the last 4 trading days. **Note**: This protective stop **does not change** until it is replaced by the trailing profit stop or a reverse entry stop.

   Remember to continue entering the opposite entry orders as described in #2 until you are no longer in the trade entry window. Should you have already entered a long trade via #2 and the short entry price is greater than either the protective stop or the profit stop, replace the protective stop price or profit stop price with the short entry price, thus exiting the current long trade and entering a new short trade. Should you have already entered a short trade via #2 and the long entry price is less than either the protective stop or the profit stop, replace the protective stop price or the profit stop

54

price with the long entry price, thus exiting the current short trade and entering a new long trade.

4. If long: When the low of the last 14 trading days is equal to or greater than the entry price, move the stop up to 1 tick (0.01 cents) below the 14-day low. As the 14-day low increases, this stop price is raised.

    If short: When the high of the last 14 trading days is equal to or less than the entry price, move the stop down to 1 tick (0.01 cents) above the 14-day high. As the 14-day high decreases, this stop price is lowered.

5. If stopped out while still in the trade entry window, go back to #2 and enter new entry orders.

6. Exit this trade on the close of the first trading day after August 12th.

Historical Results of Bean Oil Trade #1
September (U) Soybean Oil

BO		ENTRY DATE	L / S	ENTRY PRICE	EXIT DATE	EXIT METHOD	EXIT PRICE	TRADE P/L	YEARLY P/L
1960	U	05/31/60	L	8.28	08/15/60	DATEX	9.26	$588	$588
1961	U	05/23/61	S	11.42	07/03/61	PS	11.27	$90	
	U	07/14/61	S	10.42	07/25/61	PROT	10.94	-$312	-$222
1962	U	05/22/62	S	8.95	07/25/62	REV	8.32	$378	
	U	07/25/62	L	8.32	08/13/62	DATEX	8.14	-$108	$270
1963	U	05/27/63	S	9.12	07/01/63	REV	9.27	-$90	
	U	07/01/63	L	9.27	07/15/63	REV	9.01	-$156	
	U	07/15/63	S	9.01	08/13/63	DATEX	8.18	$498	$252
1964	U	06/05/64	S	8.13	07/09/64	REV	8.15	-$12	
	U	07/09/64	L	8.15	08/13/64	DATEX	8.63	$288	$276
1965	U	05/24/65	S	9.14	06/24/65	REV	9.41	-$162	
	U	06/24/65	L	9.41	08/13/65	DATEX	9.37	-$24	-$186
1966	U	06/06/66	S	10.85	06/20/66	PROT	11.18	-$198	
	U	06/20/66	L	11.22	08/15/66	DATEX	13.70	$1,488	$1,290
1967	U	05/23/67	L	10.39	05/29/67	PROT	10.20	-$114	
	U	06/01/67	S	10.19	06/05/67	PROT	10.50	-$186	
	U	06/05/67	L	10.50	06/08/67	REV	10.18	-$192	
	U	06/08/67	S	10.18	08/04/67	PS	9.26	$552	$60
1968	U	05/23/68	S	8.36	08/13/68	DATEX	7.13	$738	$738
1969	U	05/23/69	S	7.40	06/19/69	REV	7.50	-$60	
	U	06/19/69	L	7.50	08/13/69	DATEX	8.04	$324	$264
1970	U	05/22/70	L	10.79	06/26/70	REV	10.10	-$414	
	U	06/26/70	S	10.10	07/20/70	REV	10.85	-$450	
	U	07/20/70	L	10.85	08/13/70	DATEX	10.73	-$72	-$936
1971	U	05/25/71	L	11.46	08/12/71	PS	13.74	$1,368	$1,368
1972	U	05/26/72	S	11.15	07/10/72	PS	10.80	$210	
	U	07/25/72	S	10.05	08/04/72	PROT	10.44	-$234	-$24
1973	U	05/22/73	L	16.30	08/13/73	DATEX	32.95	$9,990	$9,990
1974	U	05/29/74	L	25.66	08/13/74	DATEX	41.83	$9,702	$9,702
1975	U	05/28/75	S	20.25	06/23/75	REV	21.30	-$630	
	U	06/23/75	L	21.30	08/13/75	DATEX	27.90	$3,960	$3,330
1976	U	05/24/76	L	16.77	07/22/76	REV	19.39	$1,572	
	U	07/22/76	S	19.39	08/13/76	DATEX	20.45	-$636	$936
1977	U	05/26/77	L	31.06	06/09/77	REV	28.89	-$1,302	

BO		ENTRY DATE	L / S	ENTRY PRICE	EXIT DATE	EXIT METHOD	EXIT PRICE	TRADE P/L	YEARLY P/L
	U	06/09/77	S	28.89	08/15/77	DATEX	19.30	$5,754	$4,452
1978	U	05/24/78	L	25.81	06/12/78	PROT	24.74	-$642	
	U	06/13/78	S	24.64	08/14/78	PS	23.61	$618	-$24
1979	U	05/22/79	L	26.70	05/29/79	PROT	26.05	-$390	
	U	06/11/79	L	26.71	07/25/79	PS	27.21	$300	
	U	07/27/79	S	27.04	08/13/79	DATEX	26.75	$174	$84
1980	U	05/22/80	L	22.45	08/13/80	DATEX	26.88	$2,658	$2,658
1981	U	05/26/81	S	24.14	07/08/81	PS	23.71	$258	
	U	07/09/81	L	24.11	07/31/81	REV	22.84	-$762	
	U	07/31/81	S	22.84	08/13/81	DATEX	21.40	$864	$360
1982	U	05/27/82	S	20.54	08/13/82	DATEX	17.05	$2,094	$2,094
1983	U	05/24/83	S	19.29	07/06/83	REV	19.76	-$282	
	U	07/06/83	L	19.76	08/15/83	DATEX	30.09	$6,198	$5,916
1984	U	06/04/84	S	32.59	08/13/84	DATEX	27.38	$3,126	$3,126
1985	U	06/04/85	S	27.49	06/06/85	PROT	28.20	-$426	
	U	06/07/85	L	29.10	07/01/85	REV	27.44	-$996	
	U	07/01/85	S	27.44	08/13/85	DATEX	22.49	$2,970	$1,548
1986	U	06/02/86	S	17.59	07/16/86	PS	17.11	$288	
	U	07/25/86	S	16.16	08/13/86	DATEX	14.23	$1,158	$1,446
1987	U	06/15/87	L	17.51	06/22/87	PROT	16.75	-$456	
	U	06/22/87	S	16.50	08/13/87	DATEX	15.45	$630	$174
1988	U	05/25/88	L	25.56	07/12/88	PS	29.69	$2,478	
	U	07/20/88	S	29.56	08/15/88	DATEX	27.69	$1,122	$3,600
1989	U	05/23/89	S	22.40	07/05/89	REV	22.40	$0	
	U	07/05/89	L	22.40	07/11/89	PROT	20.54	-$1,116	
	U	07/11/89	S	20.54	08/14/89	DATEX	17.71	$1,698	$582
1990	U	05/29/90	S	22.90	06/06/90	PROT	23.66	-$456	
	U	06/08/90	L	24.36	07/23/90	REV	23.32	-$624	
	U	07/23/90	S	23.32	07/27/90	PROT	23.87	-$330	-$1,338
1991	U	06/12/91	S	20.06	07/23/91	PS	19.40	$396	
	U	07/25/91	L	19.66	08/13/91	DATEX	19.63	-$18	$378
1992	U	05/29/92	L	21.73	06/23/92	REV	20.76	-$582	
	U	06/23/92	S	20.76	06/25/92	PROT	21.26	-$300	
	U	06/29/92	S	20.75	08/13/92	DATEX	18.32	$1,458	$576
1993	U	06/02/93	S	21.21	06/21/93	REV	21.95	-$444	
	U	06/21/93	L	21.95	07/26/93	PS	23.94	$1,194	
	U	07/28/93	S	23.29	08/13/93	DATEX	23.24	$30	$780
1994	U	06/06/94	S	27.14	08/08/94	PS	24.66	$1,488	$1,488

BO		ENTRY DATE	L / S	ENTRY PRICE	EXIT DATE	EXIT METHOD	EXIT PRICE	TRADE P/L	YEARLY P/L
1995	U	05/26/95	L	26.41	06/12/95	PROT	25.30	-$666	
	U	06/19/95	L	26.76	07/27/95	PS	26.89	$78	-$588
1996	U	05/29/96	S	26.89	07/11/96	PS	26.21	$408	
	U	07/12/96	L	26.58	07/22/96	REV	24.55	-$1,218	
	U	07/22/96	S	24.55	08/13/96	DATEX	25.49	-$546	-$1,374
1997	U	06/09/97	S	23.54	08/13/97	DATEX	22.03	$906	$906
1998	U	05/22/98	S	27.36	07/08/98	PS	26.55	$486	
	U	07/08/98	L	26.56	07/13/98	PROT	25.44	-$672	
	U	07/13/98	S	25.24	08/13/98	DATEX	23.54	$1,032	$846
1999	U	05/24/99	S	17.55	07/23/99	PS	16.61	$564	
	U	07/27/99	S	15.25	08/03/99	PROT	16.62	-$822	-$258
2000	U	05/30/00	S	16.65	08/14/00	DATEX	15.29	$816	$816
2001	U	05/29/01	S	14.80	05/29/01	PROT	15.08	-$168	
	U	06/01/01	L	15.46	08/13/01	DATEX	19.30	$2,304	$2,136
2002	U	05/22/02	L	17.88	08/13/02	DATEX	20.62	$1,644	$1,644

EXIT LEGEND:
DATEX = Exit Date
PROT = Protective Stop
PS = Profit Stop
REV = Reverse Entry

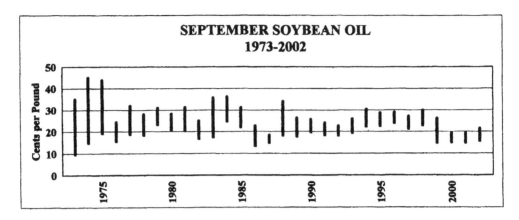

You can see from this chart that September Soybean Oil has been in a long-term consolidation. The low boundary is around 15 cents per pound and the high boundary is in the 30 cents per pound area. Historically, long trades entered above 26 cents per pound and short entries below 15 cents per pound have fared poorly.

At the end of each trade is a long-term chart. It's extremely helpful to know where the present price of the commodity is in relation to the long-term. I wouldn't expect to hit a home run with a long trade entered near the top of the trading range, and likewise I wouldn't expect a home run from a short trade entered near the bottom of the trading range.

- Chapter 5 -

LIVE CATTLE

Product Information:

Cattle were first brought to the Western Hemisphere by Christopher Columbus in 1493. These cattle were all-purpose cattle, supplying meat, milk and hides. Later, cattle breeding resulted in more specialized types of cattle, bred for their ability to quickly mature or to produce greater quantities of milk.

By the 1860's, the Corn Belt states had a fully developed cattle industry. The Great Plains and Mountain states were just beginning to enter the business.

The production of beef cattle consists of three steps: 1) Breeding and Birthing, 2) Ranching, and finally on to 3) specialized Confinement Feedlots.

Market Information:

The Chicago Mercantile Exchange began trading futures contracts on Live Cattle in 1964. This was the very first "live" contract to be traded by any futures exchange. Live Cattle's trading symbol is "LC" and the months traded are February, April, June, August, October and December. In 1984, the Mercantile Exchange began trading options on these futures contracts.

Demand Information:

Demand for beef is fairly inelastic. Lately, the per capita demand for beef has been decreasing. However, since the population has been increasing, the demand continues to remain strong. One major variable is the general state of the economy. Beef, in relation to chicken, is expensive. A poor economy will decrease the demand for beef, while a buoyant economy will increase the demand.

Supply Information:

The supply of cattle is determined by the size of the calf crop, cattle inventories and slaughter weights. Each of these are dependent on the weather in the Midwest and the price of feed. The cattle industry routinely goes through a nine-year "boom and bust" cycle. When the price of cattle gets too low, the feedlots cut their herds. After cutting the size of the herd, prices rally. As the prices rally, feedlots begin to increase the size of their herds. And as the size of the cattle crop increases, the price drops and the cycle begins again.

Reports:

The Cattle on Feed

Cold Storage

Livestock Slaughter

61

LIVE CATTLE TRADE #1

Fundamental Commentary:

After the Thanksgiving Day holiday people tire of turkey and demand red meat. As the demand for cattle increases, weather conditions often inhibit cattle marketing. Here we have the classic set-up for a rally, rising demand and fear of low supply. This is the perfect set-up for Live Cattle Trade #1 to make profits, and Live Cattle Trade #1 does just that.

Performance History

1966-2002

Total Years Examined	37	
Profitable Years	24	(77%)
Losing Years	7	(23%)
Inactive Years	6	

1973-2002

Total Net Profit	$33,290
Average Profit	$2,051
Average Loss	$603
Profit-to-Loss Ratio	3.4
Total Profits/Total Losses	10.2
Average Yearly "SUMM" Percent Profit	20.2%
Home Run Percentage	37.5%

Performance Commentary:

This trade is one of my oldest and most favorite trades. It has a long history (37 years) of producing large profits while risking only a relatively small amount

62

per contract. All the pertinent performance numbers are excellent. One thing to note about this trade is that, historically, home runs often run in groups of two (1978 and 1979, 1982 and 1983, and 1987 and 1988). This should continue, since changes in cattle production move very slowly.

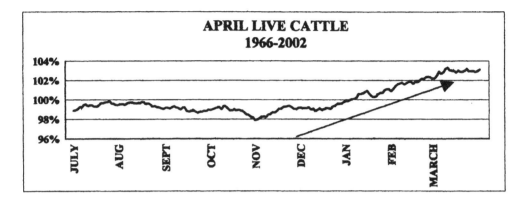

Chart Comments:

Set-up:

Normally, April Live Cattle is in a loose downtrend channel that bottoms out as early as September to as late as January, although November or December are the most common months for bottoming. After bottoming, the market begins to retrace the loss, often making new highs. This trade has one very special attribute. Every few years April Live Cattle bottoms out by making a new low in December and then quickly reverses and begins a strong uptrend. While you might be able to jump in on this trade early when this bottoming formation begins, I prefer to wait and follow the trading rules, knowing in advance that excellent profits are down the road. I wish all seasonal trades were this easy to validate!

After Entry:

After entry the cattle market begins a long and meandering up move, stopping and starting over and over again. It's not unusual for the trade to get stopped into the market and then return to a multi-day to multi-week consolidation. Some days the trade will be in profit and others in a slight loss. This is the way the cattle market trades. It trends, but slow and strong, not rapid and crazy. Trading the cattle market takes a little patience, but it's worth the wait.

Topping:

The Live Cattle market tops out in March with a consolidation period that is slow to develop. Often this happens around the time of "The Cattle on Feed Report" in mid-March.

Rules for Live Cattle Trade #1

1. Enters long April Live Cattle from the second trading day of December through the first trading day of February.

2. Place a long entry stop 1 tick (0.025 cents) above the high of the last 25 trading days. Move the entry stop as the 25-day high changes.

3. Place a protective stop 1 tick (0.025 cents) under the low of the last 2 trading days. **Note**: This protective stop **does not change** until it is replaced by the trailing profit stop.

4. When the low of the last 22 trading days is equal to or greater than the entry price, move the stop up to 1 tick (0.025 cents) below the 22-day low. As the 22-day low increases, this stop price is raised.

5. If stopped out while still in the trade entry window, go back to #2 and enter new entry orders.

6. Exit this trade on the close of the first trading day after March 23rd.

Historical Results of Live Cattle Trade #1
April (J) Live Cattle

LC		ENTRY DATE	L / S	ENTRY PRICE	EXIT DATE	EXIT METHOD	EXIT PRICE	TRADE P/L	YEARLY P/L
1966	J	12/02/65	L	26.075	03/24/66	DATEX	28.350	$910	$910
1967	J	01/09/67	L	27.675	01/12/67	PROT	27.325	-$140	-$140
1968	J	01/18/68	L	25.225	03/25/68	DATEX	27.000	$710	$710
1969	J	12/10/68	L	27.000	03/24/69	DATEX	31.975	$1,990	$1,990
1970	J	12/02/69	L	30.075	03/24/70	DATEX	32.250	$870	$870
1971	J	12/21/70	L	29.375	01/11/71	PROT	28.825	-$220	
	J	01/14/71	L	29.725	03/24/71	DATEX	32.975	$1,300	$1,080
1972	J	12/20/71	L	33.175	03/06/72	PS	33.975	$320	$320
1973	J	12/04/72	L	38.425	03/26/73	DATEX	45.575	$2,860	$2,860
1974	J	12/31/73	L	50.400	02/05/74	PS	51.725	$530	$530
1975	N/T								
1976	J	12/03/75	L	43.675	12/09/75	PROT	42.175	-$600	-$600
1977	N/T								
1978	J	12/05/77	L	40.025	03/27/78	DATEX	53.975	$5,580	$5,580
1979	J	12/04/78	L	61.000	03/26/79	DATEX	74.950	$5,580	$5,580
1980	N/T								
1981	N/T								
1982	J	01/14/82	L	59.425	03/24/82	DATEX	67.875	$3,380	$3,380
1983	J	12/23/82	L	59.650	03/24/83	DATEX	68.350	$3,480	$3,480
1984	J	12/07/83	L	65.875	01/25/84	PS	66.525	$260	$260
1985	J	01/29/85	L	68.575	02/12/85	PROT	67.125	-$580	-$580
1986	J	01/27/86	L	64.000	01/30/86	PROT	61.950	-$820	-$820
1987	J	01/09/87	L	58.025	03/24/87	DATEX	67.400	$3,750	$3,750
1988	J	12/30/87	L	65.275	03/24/88	DATEX	74.400	$3,650	$3,650
1989	J	12/21/88	L	75.325	01/18/89	PROT	74.600	-$290	
	J	01/31/89	L	76.525	03/27/89	DATEX	78.150	$650	$360
1990	J	12/26/89	L	75.075	02/21/90	PS	75.900	$330	$330
1991	J	12/10/90	L	76.775	01/09/91	PROT	75.700	-$430	
	J	01/24/91	L	77.275	03/25/91	DATEX	80.650	$1,350	$920
1992	J	01/14/92	L	75.000	01/14/92	PROT	74.475	-$210	
	J	01/21/92	L	75.375	03/24/92	DATEX	77.750	$950	$740
1993	J	12/07/92	L	74.675	03/24/93	DATEX	82.725	$3,220	$3,220
1994	J	01/07/94	L	76.275	02/03/94	PROT	75.025	-$500	-$500
1995	J	12/12/94	L	70.225	02/02/95	PS	72.925	$1,080	$1,080
1996	N/T								

66

LC		ENTRY DATE	L / S	ENTRY PRICE	EXIT DATE	EXIT METHOD	EXIT PRICE	TRADE P/L	YEARLY P/L
1997	J	12/30/96	L	65.950	01/07/97	PROT	65.225	-$290	
	J	01/10/97	L	66.475	02/06/97	PROT	65.250	-$490	-$780
1998		N/T							
1999	J	01/08/99	L	65.450	03/24/99	DATEX	66.625	$470	$470
2000	J	01/06/00	L	71.925	01/28/00	PROT	71.075	-$340	-$340
2001	J	12/04/00	L	76.525	01/26/01	PS	77.700	$470	$470
2002	J	12/24/01	L	73.300	02/26/02	PS	73.925	$250	$250

EXIT LEGEND:

DATEX = Exit Date
PROT = Protective Stop
PS = Profit Stop
REV = Reverse Entry

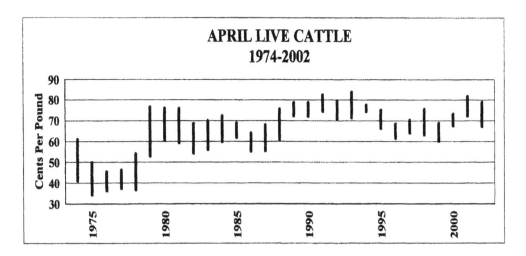

Since the mid-1980's, April Cattle have held in a tight trading range, with a bottom in the mid-50's and a top in the low 80's. This is common for the Cattle market. One day the top will be penetrated, and a trading range will be developed. The most profitable trades begin in the lower end of the range.

- Chapter 6 -

CORN

Product Information:

Corn, the largest of the cereal grains, is a member of the grass family. The cornstalk, from which the corn cob grows, bears an amazing likeness to bamboo. Each corn plant has male and female parts. This allows the plant to self pollinate. Corn grows best in rich, dark soil with warm temperatures and sufficient rainfall. This makes the Midwestern United States perfect for growing the valuable plant. This is why the Midwest is nicknamed "The Corn Belt."

Corn is one of the most important economic crops in the United States. It is the leading feed grain produced in the United States, and one of the leading agricultural exports.

Market Information:

Corn is one of the oldest trading vehicles on the Chicago Board of Trade. It began trading in 1877. The Chicago Board of Trade contract is 5,000 bushels. The trading symbol is "C." The contract months traded are March, May, July, September and December. The Chicago Board of Trade also trades options on corn futures.

Demand Information:

The demand side of the corn market is driven by the need for animal feed (mostly hogs and cattle) and for export. Two other corn products that have been gaining in importance lately are corn sweetener and the gasoline additive ethanol.

Supply Information:

Corn is grown in the Southern and Midwestern regions of the United States. The size of the crop is determined mostly by the weather conditions in these regions. The crop can be greatly damaged by a drought or heat wave striking during the silking stage of the corn (July and August). After the silking stage, the crop is considered "made" and is relatively safe from damage.

Reports:

Crop Production

Crop Progress

Export Sales

Grain Stocks

Supply & Demand Estimates

Prospective Plantings

CORN TRADE #1

Fundamental Commentary:

From planting time in mid-April, through growing time in June and silking time in July, the corn market is at risk. Weather conditions propel the market from down to up and back again, forming a multi-month price consolidation range. Eventually, after fears begin to subside and traders get a more confident guesstimate on the size of the eventual crop, the corn market begins to trend downward. Corn Trade #1 joins this falling market to make significant profits.

Performance History

1960-2002

Total Years Examined	43	
Profitable Years	28	(74%)
Losing Years	10	(26%)
Inactive Years	5	

1973-2002

Total Net Profit	$18,942
Average Profit	$1,068
Average Loss	$497
Profit-to-Loss Ratio	2.15
Total Profits/Total Losses	6.45
Average Yearly "SUMM" Percent Profit	7.9%
Home Run Percentage	29.0%

72

Performance Commentary:

This is one of my all time favorite trades. It was the first one I discovered and has helped build my personal trading account for over 20 years. This is a strong, robust trade with a long history of profits, a good profit-to-loss ratio and a nearly 30% chance of a home run. It's trades like this that take accounts to new equity heights.

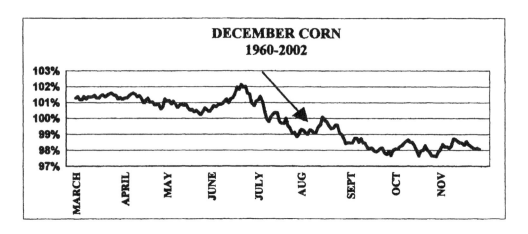

Chart Comments:

Set-up:

From the first of the year through April, December Corn is normally trapped in a wide consolidation range. At times there is a slightly upward bias, and at other times there is a slightly downward bias. During May expect a mild rally that may appear to be a breakout from the trading range. Don't be fooled, this rally almost always fades and prices begin to descend. At this point, Corn Trade #1's entry stop is activated and the trade is entered.

After Entry:

This trade begins earning paper profits quickly but often stalls around the Fourth of July. At this time, a rally usually develops. The trade may be stopped out with this rally. Should the crop be in danger due to bad weather conditions, this rally could turn into a major counter-seasonal rally. If you are stopped out, remember to place the trade's entry stop with your broker. If the rally fails, the downtrend will continue.

Bottoming:

From mid to late July, December Corn begins to form a long consolidation range. The narrowness of this range depends on the size and speed of the previous price decline. A fast, steep decline in prices typically results in the bottom exhibiting wide swings. On the other hand, should the decline be slow, expect a narrow consolidation range to develop. If the downtrend has been of short duration, and the price decline only moderate, there may be enough buying pressure to form a "V" shaped bottom.

Rules for Corn Trade #1

1. Enters short December Corn from the first trading day after May 12th through the first trading day of August.

2. Place a short entry stop 1 tick (0.25 cents) below the low of the last 21 trading days. Move the entry stop as the 21-day low changes.

3. Place a protective stop 1 tick (0.25 cents) above the high of the last 2 trading days. **Note:** This protective stop **does not change** until it is replaced by the trailing profit stop.

4. When the high of the last 11 trading days is equal to or less than the entry price, move the stop down to 1 tick (0.25 cents) above the 11-day high. As the 11-day high decreases, this stop price is lowered.

5. If stopped out while still in the trade entry window, go back to #2 and enter new entry orders.

6. Exit this trade on the close of the first trading day after August 6th.

Historical Results of Corn Trade #1
December (Z) Corn

C		ENTRY DATE	L / S	ENTRY PRICE	EXIT DATE	EXIT METHOD	EXIT PRICE	TRADE P/L	YEARLY P/L
1960		N/T							
1961	Z	05/23/61	S	118.50	06/01/61	PROT	122.00	-$175	
	Z	06/19/61	S	118.25	06/30/61	PROT	120.25	-$100	
	Z	07/21/61	S	118.25	08/07/61	DATEX	115.00	$163	-$112
1962	Z	05/23/62	S	117.25	08/07/62	DATEX	105.50	$588	$588
1963	Z	05/22/63	S	113.00	05/22/63	PROT	115.25	-$113	
	Z	07/15/63	S	115.25	08/07/63	DATEX	111.50	$188	$75
1964	Z	05/14/64	S	117.25	05/22/64	PROT	118.50	-$63	
	Z	06/09/64	S	117.00	08/03/64	PS	115.75	$63	$0
1965	Z	05/17/65	S	119.25	06/16/65	PROT	120.25	-$50	
	Z	07/12/65	S	118.25	07/22/65	PROT	119.75	-$75	-$125
1966		N/T							
1967	Z	05/17/66	S	133.25	05/26/67	PROT	136.50	-$163	
	Z	06/15/67	S	130.75	08/07/67	DATEX	119.50	$563	$400
1968	Z	05/21/68	S	118.50	05/31/68	PROT	120.50	-$100	
	Z	06/05/68	S	118.25	06/06/68	PROT	120.00	-$88	
	Z	06/17/68	S	118.00	08/07/68	DATEX	105.00	$650	$462
1969	Z	06/11/69	S	122.75	06/23/69	PROT	125.75	-$150	
	Z	07/25/69	S	119.25	08/07/69	DATEX	115.75	$175	$25
1970	Z	07/28/70	S	127.50	08/07/70	DATEX	129.75	-$113	-$113
1971	Z	07/06/71	S	145.25	08/09/71	DATEX	123.25	$1,100	$1,100
1972	Z	05/15/72	S	126.00	06/30/72	PS	123.00	$150	$150
1973		N/T							
1974		N/T							
1975	Z	05/28/75	S	237.50	06/17/75	PROT	250.75	-$663	
	Z	06/30/75	S	234.00	07/08/75	PROT	246.50	-$625	-$1,288
1976	Z	07/22/76	S	272.50	08/09/76	DATEX	267.50	$250	$250
1977	Z	05/20/77	S	245.25	05/24/77	PROT	251.50	-$313	
	Z	06/09/77	S	244.25	08/08/77	DATEX	204.25	$2,000	$1,687
1978	Z	06/15/78	S	254.50	08/07/78	DATEX	221.75	$1,638	$1,638
1979	Z	07/26/79	S	295.75	08/07/79	DATEX	273.50	$1,113	$1,113
1980	Z	06/02/80	S	292.00	06/16/80	PROT	295.75	-$188	-$188
1981	Z	05/21/81	S	363.00	07/13/81	PROT	372.50	-$475	
	Z	08/03/81	S	341.75	08/07/81	DATEX	330.50	$563	$88

C		ENTRY DATE	L / S	ENTRY PRICE	EXIT DATE	EXIT METHOD	EXIT PRICE	TRADE P/L	YEARLY P/L
1982	Z	05/25/82	S	282.00	08/09/82	DATEX	245.50	$1,825	$1,825
1983	Z	05/16/83	S	286.25	06/22/83	PS	280.50	$288	
	Z	07/05/83	S	272.00	07/07/83	PROT	281.75	-$488	-$200
1984	Z	07/05/84	S	294.25	08/07/84	DATEX	280.75	$675	$675
1985	Z	05/16/85	S	261.00	06/07/85	PS	259.50	$75	
	Z	06/20/85	S	250.75	06/20/85	PROT	253.25	-$125	
	Z	06/21/85	S	250.50	06/21/85	PROT	253.50	-$150	
	Z	07/01/85	S	250.00	08/07/85	DATEX	225.25	$1,238	$1,038
1986	Z	05/29/86	S	193.75	06/03/86	PROT	197.00	-$163	
	Z	06/12/86	S	192.25	08/07/86	DATEX	168.50	$1,188	$1,025
1987	Z	07/01/87	S	188.75	08/07/87	DATEX	163.75	$1,250	$1,250
1988	Z	07/20/88	S	308.75	08/08/88	DATEX	304.50	$213	$213
1989	Z	05/16/89	S	256.75	06/14/89	PS	241.50	$763	
	Z	07/18/89	S	238.75	08/07/89	DATEX	226.75	$600	$1,363
1990	Z	06/04/90	S	264.75	06/05/90	PROT	270.25	-$275	
	Z	07/09/90	S	271.50	08/07/90	DATEX	249.25	$1,113	$838
1991	Z	05/30/91	S	241.25	06/03/91	PROT	248.25	-$350	
	Z	06/17/91	S	239.75	06/19/91	PROT	243.25	-$175	
	Z	06/21/91	S	236.75	07/16/91	PS	236.75	$0	-$525
1992	Z	06/23/92	S	254.00	06/23/92	PROT	260.00	-$300	
	Z	07/06/92	S	249.00	08/07/92	DATEX	214.50	$1,725	$1,425
1993	Z	06/01/93	S	234.50	06/30/93	PROT	238.25	-$188	-$188
1994	Z	06/22/94	S	249.00	08/08/94	PS	223.25	$1,288	$1,288
1995	Z	06/27/95	S	272.50	07/06/95	PROT	289.75	-$863	-$863
1996	Z	07/18/96	S	345.75	08/07/96	DATEX	321.00	$1,238	$1,238
1997	Z	05/13/97	S	265.75	07/14/97	PS	248.00	$888	$888
1998	Z	05/20/98	S	256.75	06/17/98	PS	250.00	$338	
	Z	07/14/98	S	237.75	08/07/98	DATEX	221.00	$838	$1,176
1999	Z	05/24/99	S	229.50	05/28/99	PROT	234.00	-$225	
	Z	06/24/99	S	224.00	07/21/99	PS	212.25	$588	$363
2000	Z	05/25/00	S	249.50	08/07/00	DATEX	190.00	$2,975	$2,975
2001	Z	05/21/01	S	214.75	07/03/01	PS	213.50	$63	$63
2002	Z	06/11/02	S	220.25	06/12/02	PROT	224.75	-$225	-$225

EXIT LEGEND:
DATEX = Exit Date
PROT = Protective Stop
PS = Profit Stop
REV = Reverse Entry

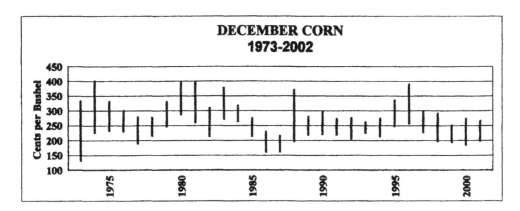

December Corn has been in a wide, long-term trading range for more than a quarter of a century. The top boundary is around $3.50 and the bottom around $1.75. I would be careful entering any shorts near the lower end of this range.

- Chapter 7 -

COTTON

Product Information:

As early as 5000 BC, cotton was cultivated in India, Egypt and China. China is the world's largest producer of cotton. Cotton needs a temperate to hot climate in which to grow, which restricts production of cotton to the southernmost states of the United States.

Market Information:

Cotton futures are traded on the New York Cotton Exchange. The trading symbol is "CT" and the months traded are March, May, July, October and December. The contract size is 50,000 lbs. The exchange also trades options of these futures.

Demand Information:

Cotton demand is directly related to the strength of the economy, although the many waves of consumer likes and dislikes also have a strong influence. At times cotton fabric is the "in" material, while at other times it's on the "outs." It all depends upon the whims of the fashion industry and the buying public.

Supply Information:

Cotton is a field crop. Like other field crops, the main concern is the weather in the cotton growing regions of the southern United States. Texas is the largest producing state.

Reports:

Crop Production

Crop Progress

Export Sales

Supply & Demand Estimates

Prospective Plantings

COTTON TRADE #1

Fundamental Commentary:

The cotton market is weather driven during the growth stages from mid-February through late June. Good weather will yield a large crop, a bulge in supply and lower prices. Bad weather has the opposite effect – a small crop, a cut in the expected supply, and higher prices. If a price rally develops, it may be steep and price appreciation can be great. That's the nature of the cotton market. If the market declines, the drop in prices will be slow and may continue for a long time. This decline also produces terrific profits for those fortunate enough to hold short positions. Cotton Trade #1 places entry orders on either side of the market, and allows the price action of the cotton market to decide the way to enter the trade, either long or short.

Performance History

1961-2002

Total Years Examined	42	
Profitable Years	29	(71%)
Losing Years	12	(29%)
Inactive Years	1	

1973-2002

Total Net Profit	$51,940
Average Profit	$2,821
Average Loss	$1,266
Profit-to-Loss Ratio	2.23
Total Profits/Total Losses	6.13
Average Yearly "SUMM" Percent Profit	11.4%
Home Run Percentage	33.3%

Performance Commentary:

Cotton Trade #1 has a long history, with a high percentage of profitable trades and a good profit-to-loss ratio. What makes this trade stand out as one I would trade every year is the high probability of hitting a home run (one out of every three years.)

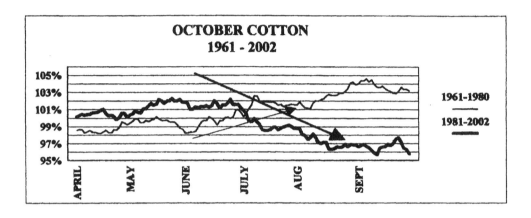

Chart Comments:

Set-up:

From January through March, October Cotton is in either a consolidation range or a downtrend. During the planting time of mid-April through May expect a rally. The rally is driven by the planting intentions report and weather conditions in the cotton growing parts of the nation. Should the weather be cold and wet, the farmers will have trouble planting the crop. The later the crop is planted, the smaller the harvest. If the weather is good, the rally won't transpire and prices will be driven downward.

After Entry:

If long, this is most likely a weather driven panic. Expect a quick violent rally that produces profits immediately. But watch out! Rain can quickly reverse this uptrend.

If short, the weather is good and the crop is on the road to a normal harvest. The prices will keep falling and profits will grow. The nearer to the late August exit date, the faster prices will decline.

Bottoming:

Around the end of August, cotton prices begin to consolidate. At times a recovery rally will follow.

Topping:

Propelled by fears of bad weather, the rally is often fast and strong. However, even the slightest hint of rain can send this volatile market down. Upside-down "V" reversals are normal.

Rules for Cotton Trade #1:

1. Enters long or short October Cotton from the first trading day after May 5th through the first trading day after July 14th.

2. Place a long entry stop 1 tick (0.01 cents) above the high of the last 31 trading days, **and** place a short entry stop 1 tick (0.01 cents) below the low of the last 31 trading days. Move these entry stops as the 31-day high and 31-day low change.

3. When filled:

    On long: Place a protective stop 1 tick (0.01 cents) under the low of the last 2 trading days. **Note**: This protective stop **does not change** until it is replaced by the trailing profit stop or a reverse entry stop.

    On short: Place a protective stop 1 tick (0.01 cents) above the high of the last 2 trading days. **Note**: This protective stop **does not change** until it is replaced by the trailing profit stop or a reverse entry stop.

Remember to continue entering the opposite entry orders as described in #2 until you are no longer in the trade entry window. Should you have already entered a long trade via #2 and the short entry price is greater than either the protective stop or the profit stop, replace the protective stop price or profit stop price with the short entry price, thus exiting the current long trade and entering a new short trade. Should you have already entered a short trade via #2 and the long entry price is less than either the protective stop or the profit stop, replace the protective stop price or the profit stop

price with the long entry price, thus exiting the current short trade and entering a new long trade.

4. If long: When the low of the last 8 trading days is equal to or greater than the entry price, move the stop up to 1 tick (0.01 cents) below the 8-day low. As the 8-day low increases, this stop price is raised.

   If short: When the high of the last 8 trading days is equal to or less than the entry price, move the stop down to 1 tick (0.01 cents) above the 8-day high. As the 8-day high decreases, this stop price is lowered.

5. If stopped out while still in the trade entry window, go back to #2 and enter new entry orders.

6. If long: Exit this trade on the close of the first day after July 20th.

   If short: Exit this trade on the close of the first day after August 22nd.

Historical Results of Cotton Trade #1
October (V) Cotton

CT		ENTRY DATE	L/S	ENTRY PRICE	EXIT DATE	EXIT METHOD	EXIT PRICE	TRADE P/L	YEARLY P/L
1961	V	06/06/61	L	34.28	06/21/61	PROT	34.04	-$120	
	V	06/21/61	S	34.00	06/30/61	PROT	34.17	-$85	-$205
1962	V	05/14/62	L	34.50	05/28/62	PS	34.53	$15	
	V	06/22/62	S	34.41	07/25/62	PS	33.94	$235	$250
1963	V	06/13/63	L	32.76	07/11/63	PS	32.97	$105	$105
1964	V	05/22/64	L	29.61	05/26/64	PROT	29.00	-$305	
	V	06/03/64	L	29.71	07/21/64	DATEX	31.25	$770	$465
1965		N/T							
1966	V	05/23/66	S	22.25	05/25/66	PROT	22.45	-$100	
	V	05/26/66	S	22.20	08/23/66	DATEX	21.75	$225	$125
1967	V	05/15/67	L	26.75	07/21/67	DATEX	28.98	$1,115	$1,115
1968	V	05/14/68	L	30.75	07/22/68	DATEX	33.25	$1,250	$1,250
1969	V	05/22/69	S	25.68	06/05/69	PS	25.68	$0	
	V	06/24/69	S	25.32	07/10/69	PROT	25.89	-$285	
	V	07/10/69	L	25.89	07/18/69	PROT	25.10	-$395	-$680
1970	V	05/28/70	L	26.09	06/25/70	PS	26.15	$30	
	V	07/13/70	L	26.66	07/20/70	PROT	26.29	-$185	-$155
1971	V	05/11/71	L	30.68	05/27/71	PS	30.81	$65	
	V	06/02/71	S	28.60	07/09/71	PROT	31.51	-$1,455	
	V	07/14/71	L	31.96	07/19/71	PROT	31.26	-$350	-$1,740
1972	V	05/17/72	S	34.85	07/21/72	PS	31.47	$1,690	$1,690
1973	V	05/08/73	L	50.06	05/15/73	PROT	47.49	-$1,285	
	V	06/04/73	L	51.76	06/07/73	PROT	49.49	-$1,135	
	V	06/27/73	L	53.21	07/23/73	DATEX	64.90	$5,845	$3,425
1974	V	05/07/74	S	53.99	06/05/74	PS	52.00	$995	
	V	07/08/74	L	56.01	07/09/74	PROT	53.69	-$1,160	-$165
1975	V	05/08/75	L	48.36	05/14/75	PROT	46.74	-$810	
	V	05/28/75	S	44.84	06/10/75	PROT	46.56	-$860	
	V	06/24/75	L	47.99	07/16/75	PS	48.04	$25	-$1,645
1976	V	05/14/76	L	66.81	05/18/76	PROT	64.24	-$1,285	
	V	05/26/76	L	67.18	07/15/76	PS	86.29	$9,555	$8,270
1977	V	05/17/77	S	70.29	06/24/77	PS	63.81	$3,240	
	V	07/08/77	S	59.84	08/23/77	DATEX	54.62	$2,610	$5,850
1978	V	05/09/78	L	61.66	05/30/78	PS	62.10	$220	

CT		ENTRY DATE	L/S	ENTRY PRICE	EXIT DATE	EXIT METHOD	EXIT PRICE	TRADE P/L	YEARLY P/L
	V	06/27/78	S	60.49	07/14/78	PS	60.41	$40	$260
1979	V	05/29/79	S	61.20	05/29/79	PROT	62.01	-$405	
	V	06/08/79	L	65.41	06/27/79	PS	66.39	$490	$85
1980	V	05/27/80	S	74.58	06/18/80	PS	72.81	$885	
	V	07/07/80	L	78.10	07/23/80	DATEX	79.75	$825	$1,710
1981	V	05/11/81	S	81.19	06/01/81	PROT	82.86	-$835	
	V	06/03/81	S	80.19	07/06/81	PS	79.96	$115	
	V	07/13/81	S	77.39	08/24/81	DATEX	66.00	$5,695	$4,975
1982	V	05/14/82	S	70.34	06/21/82	PS	67.86	$1,240	
	V	06/29/82	L	70.91	07/21/82	DATEX	71.42	$255	$1,495
1983	V	05/09/83	L	74.41	06/15/83	PS	77.00	$1,295	
	V	06/21/83	L	79.81	07/01/83	PROT	76.94	-$1,435	-$140
1984	V	05/08/84	L	80.50	05/11/84	PROT	79.44	-$530	
	V	05/21/84	L	80.61	06/04/84	PROT	78.45	-$1,080	
	V	06/08/84	S	77.64	08/03/84	PS	67.50	$5,070	$3,460
1985	V	05/07/85	S	64.14	06/13/85	PS	62.06	$1,040	$1,040
1986	V	05/27/86	S	35.59	07/23/86	PS	31.21	$2,190	$2,190
1987	V	05/07/87	L	65.21	06/02/87	PS	69.17	$1,980	
	V	06/15/87	L	74.31	07/21/87	DATEX	76.38	$1,035	$3,015
1988	V	05/13/88	L	60.76	06/24/88	PS	64.10	$1,670	
	V	07/05/88	S	60.19	08/23/88	DATEX	50.40	$4,895	$6,565
1989	V	05/12/89	L	68.30	06/05/89	PS	66.79	-$755	
	V	06/06/89	S	65.14	06/13/89	PROT	69.54	-$2,200	
	V	06/13/89	L	69.54	07/21/89	DATEX	73.57	$2,015	-$940
1990	V	05/09/90	L	70.51	07/09/90	PS	77.24	$3,365	$3,365
1991	V	05/09/91	L	79.01	06/03/91	PROT	76.83	-$1,090	
	V	06/25/91	S	76.62	07/23/91	PS	71.41	$2,605	$1,515
1992	V	05/14/92	L	63.59	05/19/92	PROT	60.39	-$1,600	
	V	05/20/92	S	60.15	06/09/92	PROT	63.08	-$1,465	
	V	06/12/92	L	64.30	07/21/92	DATEX	62.82	-$740	-$3,805
1993	V	05/17/93	S	60.69	07/09/93	PS	58.01	$1,340	
	V	07/12/93	L	60.11	07/21/93	DATEX	61.60	$745	$2,085
1994	V	05/19/94	L	76.61	06/08/94	PS	77.12	$225	
	V	06/27/94	S	74.32	07/22/94	PS	72.01	$1,155	$1,410
1995	V	05/11/95	L	87.78	05/31/95	PROT	84.09	-$1,845	
	V	06/08/95	L	91.50	07/06/95	PROT	83.09	-$4,205	
	V	07/06/95	S	82.34	08/14/95	PS	75.08	$3,630	-$2,420
1996	V	05/10/96	S	81.49	07/19/96	PS	73.91	$3,790	$3,790

88

CT		ENTRY DATE	L / S	ENTRY PRICE	EXIT DATE	EXIT METHOD	EXIT PRICE	TRADE P/L	YEARLY P/L
1997	V	05/29/97	L	75.11	07/07/97	PROT	73.99	-$560	
	V	07/07/97	S	73.64	08/25/97	DATEX	73.10	$270	-$290
1998	V	05/22/98	L	69.76	06/11/98	PS	72.68	$1,460	
	V	06/22/98	L	77.11	07/10/98	PS	77.54	$215	$1,675
1999	V	05/20/99	S	57.69	07/21/99	PS	51.26	$3,215	$3,215
2000	V	05/10/00	L	61.40	05/31/00	PS	62.45	$525	
	V	05/31/00	L	65.50	06/01/00	PROT	62.65	-$1,425	
	V	06/27/00	S	56.90	07/13/00	PS	56.55	$175	-$725
2001	V	05/09/01	S	48.30	05/15/01	PROT	49.40	-$550	
	V	05/16/01	S	47.35	06/07/01	PS	45.15	$1,100	
	V	06/15/01	S	42.75	07/26/01	PS	41.10	$825	$1,375
2002	V	05/31/02	L	41.00	07/16/02	PS	43.60	$1,300	$1,300

EXIT LEGEND:
DATEX = Exit Date
PROT   = Protective Stop
PS   = Profit Stop
REV   = Reverse Entry

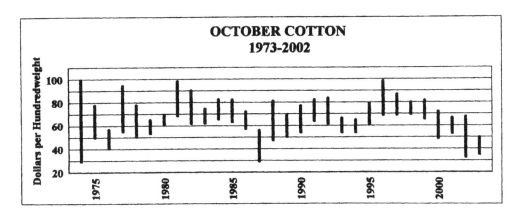

October Cotton has well defined long-term top and bottom ranges. The top range is around the 80 cent level and the bottom is in the area of 30 cents. Historically, entries above 79 cents have not proved profitable. Unfortunately, there are no danger areas on the short side of which I can warn you. I can say that I would not enter any shorts below 29 cents.

- Chapter 8 -

CRUDE OIL

Product Information:

Crude Oil (petroleum) is the lifeblood of the world's business. Its products power most of the world's machines, can be turned into unlimited plastic products and can even be used in various medicines. The world owes much to the pioneers in the early oil drilling era (circa mid 1850's).

The word "petroleum" is derived from the Latin words for "rock" and "oil." Crude oil is formed from the transformation of sediment due to extreme pressure. Most scientists believe that the world's petroleum reserve is limited, but there is a growing number of oil experts who believe that new petroleum is being formed continuously.

Market Information:

The New York Mercantile Exchange began trading Crude Oil futures contracts (1000 barrels) in 1983. The trading symbol is "CL." Crude Oil contracts are traded for each month of the year. In 1986, the New York Mercantile Exchange began trading options on the futures.

Recently, the exchange has begun trading a smaller 400 barrel contract of crude oil on the electronic exchange. This will open the trading of crude oil to the smaller investor.

Demand Information:

The Crude Oil market is demand driven. The two major products, heating oil and gasoline, are the powers behind the demand. The approach of cold weather in either hemisphere pressures the price of heating oil. In the warmer summer months, the demand for gasoline increases.

Supply Information:

The available supply of crude oil is often a political decision. Much of the available oil is in the hands of the OPEC Nations. At regular time periods they meet and set the output quotas for each of the countries in their group. This attempt at setting supply limits rarely works. The nations in OPEC have a long history of cheating on their quotas. Nations not in OPEC often increase their production to make up for the proposed decline in supply. Every year new, large fields of crude oil are being discovered.

Reports:

American Petroleum Institute's Weekly Report

CRUDE OIL TRADE #1

Fundamental Commentary:

In late February thru the month of March, the oil refineries are switching production from heating oil to gasoline in order to build up inventories for the coming driving season. This frequently causes a shortage. Crude oil demand increases and the price shows it. Crude Oil Trade #1 takes advantage of this increase to build profits.

Performance History

1984-2002

Total Years Examined	19	
Profitable Years	12	(75%)
Losing Years	4	(25%)
Inactive Years	3	

1984-2002

Total Net Profit	$21,800
Average Profit	$2,023
Average Loss	$620
Profit-to-Loss Ratio	3.3
Total Profits/Total Losses	9.8
Average Yearly "SUMM" Percent Profit	9.7%
Home Run Percentage	25.0%

Performance Commentary:

This is one of my favorite Crude Oil trades. If the current market price is in the teens, this trade can really make money. As you can see from the performance numbers, it is very reliable and has an excellent profit-to-loss ratio. Also, a home run percentage of 25% is excellent.

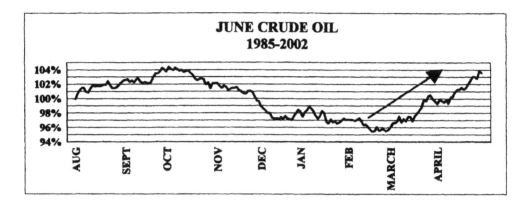

Chart Comments:

Set-up:

June Crude Oil normally forms a broad consolidation range during the later part of the year, continuing into the beginning of the next year. Then the prices begin to fall. Many times the price of crude oil makes a new seasonal low. If this is the chart set-up, get ready to earn some profits. This is a perfect set-up! The second best set-up is joining an exhausting trend. They too can bring in good profits.

After Entry:

The uptrend often is a duplicate of the preceding downtrend. If the downtrend was steep and quick, expect the same of the uptrend. If the downtrend was slow and the price decline minimal, you can expect the uptrend to be roughly the same.

Topping:

Expect a top in mid to late April. And don't be surprised if the trend ends in a reverse "V" top, particularly if the uptrend has been very strong.

Rules for Crude Oil Trade #1:

1. Enters long June Crude Oil from the first trading day after February 24th through the first trading day of April.

2. Place a long entry stop 1 tick (0.01 dollars) above the high of the last 17 trading days. Move the entry stop as the 17-day high changes.

3. Place a protective stop 1 tick (0.01 dollars) below the low of the last 3 trading days. **Note**: This protective stop **does not change** until it is replaced by the trailing profit stop.

4. When the low of the last 14 trading days is equal to or greater than the entry price, move the stop up to 1 tick (0.01 dollars) below the 14-day low. As the 14-day low increases, this stop price is raised.

5. If stopped out while still in the trade entry window, go back to #2 and enter new entry orders.

6. Exit this trade on the close of the first trading day after April 20th.

Historical Results of Crude Oil Trade #1
June (M) Crude Oil

CL		ENTRY DATE	L / S	ENTRY PRICE	EXIT DATE	EXIT METHOD	EXIT PRICE	TRADE P/L	YEARLY P/L
1984	M	02/27/84	L	29.96	04/18/84	PS	30.46	$500	$500
1985	M	03/04/85	L	26.61	04/22/85	DATEX	28.49	$1,880	$1,880
1986		N/T							
1987	M	03/09/87	L	18.01	04/21/87	DATEX	18.40	$390	$390
1988	M	03/21/88	L	16.40	04/21/88	DATEX	18.36	$1,960	$1,960
1989	M	02/27/89	L	17.36	04/21/89	DATEX	21.32	$3,960	$3,960
1990		N/T							
1991	M	03/04/91	L	19.52	04/22/91	DATEX	21.32	$1,800	$1,800
1992	M	03/12/92	L	19.13	04/21/92	DATEX	20.44	$1,310	$1,310
1993	M	02/26/93	L	20.71	03/11/93	PROT	20.38	-$330	-$330
1994	M	03/21/94	L	15.23	03/28/94	PROT	14.54	-$690	
	M	04/04/94	L	15.39	04/21/94	DATEX	16.63	$1,240	$550
1995	M	03/20/95	L	18.40	04/21/95	DATEX	20.41	$2,010	$2,010
1996	M	03/12/96	L	18.79	04/22/96	DATEX	21.53	$2,740	$2,740
1997	M	03/18/97	L	21.21	03/26/97	PROT	20.64	-$570	-$570
1998	M	03/23/98	L	17.40	04/21/98	DATEX	15.98	-$1,420	-$1,420
1999	M	03/04/99	L	13.21	04/21/99	DATEX	17.90	$4,690	$4,690
2000	M	02/25/00	L	27.46	03/20/00	PS	27.30	-$160	-$160
2001		N/T							
2002	M	02/28/02	L	22.06	04/12/02	PS	24.55	$2,490	$2,490

EXIT LEGEND:
DATEX = Exit Date
PROT = Protective Stop
PS = Profit Stop
REV = Reverse Entry

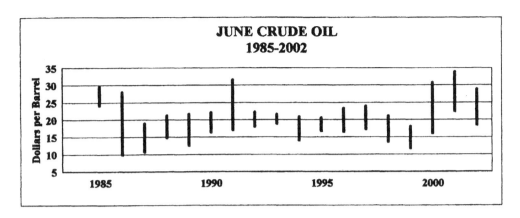

June Crude Oil hasn't been trading all that long, but it has established a strong and well formed bottoming area in the $10 to $13 a barrel range. Crude Oil Trade #1 has produced great profits entering on the two major lows. I wish the high range was as easy to detect, but it's not. Entries above $30 have proved to be profitable. I would not skip trades that are in the higher end of the trading range.

CRUDE OIL TRADE #2:

Fundamental Commentary:

From July through September the demand for crude oil increases rapidly. The refineries are producing gasoline as quickly as possible to fill the needs of the summer driving season. At the same time, orders for heating oil are beginning to stack up. This puts severe demand pressure on the crude oil market and forces prices higher. Crude Oil Trade #2 profits from this annual rally.

Performance History

1983-2002

Total Years Examined	20	
Profitable Years	14	(74%)
Losing Years	5	(26%)
Inactive Years	1	

1983-2002

Total Net Profit	$27,450
Average Profit	$2,254
Average Loss	$822
Profit-to-Loss Ratio	2.74
Total Profits/Total Losses	7.67
Average Yearly "SUMM" Percent Profit	5.7%
Home Run Percentage	5.3%

Performance Commentary:

The two numbers that stand out in the Performance History for Crude Oil Trade #2 are the excellent 2.7 to 1 profit-to-loss ratio and the total profits/total losses number of 7.7. Although this trade is open a relatively short time, the Average Yearly "SUMM" Percent Profit of 5.7% is quite good.

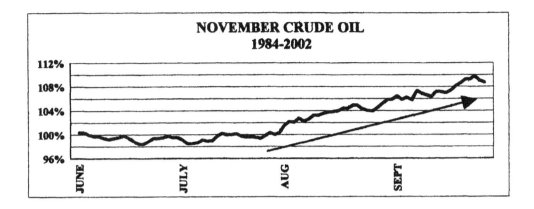

Chart Comments:

Set-up:

Look for the formation of a double bottom in June and July. At times, a third bottom may be formed in August. After these two or possibly three bottoms, and an upside breakout, most trades have been profitable. The upside reaction from this bottom is the normal entry point for this trade. The trade is rarely entered after the uptrend has begun. Two out of three of these entries are losers. If you enter with the uptrend, watch the trade closely for reversals.

After Entry:

Once the trend begins expect a short period of backing and filling before rallying to new highs. While this uptrend is normally strong, it meanders upward, forming short-term price consolidations and breaking out to the upside.

Topping:

Expect a top in mid-to-late September. Don't be surprised if the trend ends in a reverse "V" top.

Rules for Crude Oil #2:

1. Enters long November Crude Oil from the first trading day after July 24th through the first trading day after September 5th.

2. Place a long entry stop 1 tick (0.01 dollars) above the high of the last 10 trading days. Move the entry stop as the 10-day high changes.

3. Place a protective stop 1 tick (0.01 dollars) below the low of the last 3 trading days. **Note**: This protective stop **does not change** until it is replaced by the trailing profit stop.

4. When the low of the last 5 trading days is equal to or greater than the entry price, move the stop up to 1 tick (0.01 dollars) below the 5-day low. As the 5-day low increases, this stop price is raised.

5. If stopped out while still in the trade entry window, go back to #2 and enter new entry orders.

6. Exit this trade on the close of the first trading day after September 25th.

Historical Results of Crude Oil Trade #2
November (X) Crude Oil

CL		ENTRY DATE	L / S	ENTRY PRICE	EXIT DATE	EXIT METHOD	EXIT PRICE	TRADE P/L	YEARLY P/L
1983	X	07/28/83	L	31.71	08/09/83	PS	31.93	$220	$220
1984	X	08/02/84	L	29.24	08/30/84	PS	29.77	$530	$530
1985	X	07/25/85	L	26.28	09/05/85	PS	27.51	$1,230	$1,230
1986	X	08/04/86	L	12.26	09/08/86	PS	15.71	$3,450	$3,450
1987	X	08/03/87	L	21.80	08/06/87	PROT	20.65	-$1,150	-$1,150
1988		N/T							
1989	X	08/17/89	L	18.31	09/22/89	PS	19.23	$920	$920
1990	X	07/27/90	L	21.50	08/28/90	PS	26.70	$5,200	
	X	09/06/90	L	30.81	09/26/90	DATEX	38.67	$7,860	$13,060
1991	X	08/19/91	L	22.76	09/26/91	DATEX	22.21	-$550	-$550
1992	X	08/24/92	L	21.33	09/18/92	PS	21.73	$400	$400
1993	X	08/12/93	L	18.67	09/07/93	PROT	17.75	-$920	-$920
1994	X	07/28/94	L	19.08	08/05/94	PS	19.14	$60	$60
1995	X	07/26/95	L	17.24	08/28/95	PS	17.41	$170	
	X	09/05/95	L	17.92	09/20/95	PS	18.09	$170	$340
1996	X	08/02/96	L	20.21	08/26/96	PS	21.15	$940	
	X	09/03/96	L	23.10	09/26/96	DATEX	24.16	$1,060	$2,000
1997	X	07/25/97	L	20.18	08/25/97	PROT	19.55	-$630	-$630
1998	X	09/03/98	L	14.30	09/28/98	DATEX	15.64	$1,340	$1,340
1999	X	07/28/99	L	20.61	08/25/99	PS	21.22	$610	
	X	08/31/99	L	22.16	09/27/99	DATEX	24.61	$2,450	$3,060
2000	X	08/04/00	L	28.91	09/14/00	PS	32.14	$3,230	$3,230
2001	X	07/26/01	L	26.39	08/16/01	PS	26.39	$0	
	X	08/29/01	L	27.42	09/19/01	PROT	26.56	-$860	-$860
2002	X	08/14/02	L	26.95	09/03/02	PS	28.07	$1,120	
	X	09/06/02	L	29.80	09/26/02	DATEX	30.40	$600	$1,720

EXIT LEGEND:
DATEX = Exit Date
PROT = Protective Stop
PS = Profit Stop
REV = Reverse Entry

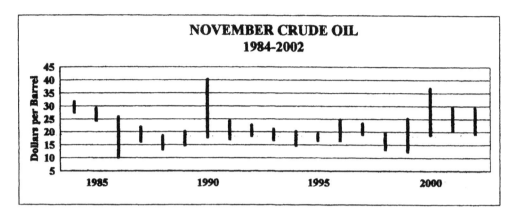

November Crude Oil hasn't been trading all that long, but it has established a strong and well formed bottoming area in the $10 to $13 a barrel range. Crude Oil Trade #2 has produced great profits entering on the two major lows. I wish the high range was as easy to detect, but it's not. Entries above $30 have proved to be profitable. I would not skip trades that are in the higher end of the trading range.

CRUDE OIL TRADE #3

Fundamental Commentary:

The supply/demand picture for Crude Oil during October through November normally shows a growing supply and a decreasing demand. Why is the supply increasing? The old Soviet Union produces a large quantity of crude oil. This oil is shipped in giant tankers. During the harsh winter the waterways freeze, and the tankers cannot move. Therefore, as much oil as possible is shipped before the winter, which causes a glut. The summer driving season is long over, and many of the orders for heating oil have already been filled. We have a classic "over supply/under demand" market which forces prices lower. Crude Oil Trade #3 profits from this decline.

Performance History

1984-2003

Total Years Examined	20	
Profitable Years	14	(78%)
Losing Years	4	(22%)
Inactive Years	2	

1984-2003

Total Net Profit	$35,710
Average Profit	$2,886
Average Loss	$1,173
Profit-to-Loss Ratio	2.5
Total Profits/Total Losses	8.6
Average Yearly "SUMM" Percent Profit	12.8%
Home Run Percentage	27.8%

Performance Commentary:

This is truly one great trade. It has everything: a high percentage of winning trades, a good profit-to-loss ratio, an excellent Average Yearly "SUMM" Percent Profit and a superior Home Run Percentage.

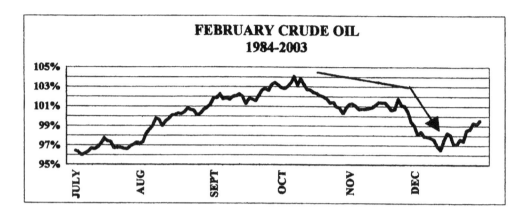

Chart Comments:

Set-up:

Crude Oil usually rallies into October and begins to form a short to long-term consolidation top. The longer the consolidation range, the greater the potential for profits. This trade is specifically designed to capture the downside breakout from the consolidation range.

After Entry:

The Crude Oil market has a strong tendency to rally after the breakout entry. It is quite rare for this short-term rally to reach the trade's protective stop. The rally will fail and the much stronger downtrend will continue.

Bottoming:

Crude Oil bottoms in mid-December, often in a "V" reversal. At this time of the year the Crude Oil market is very volatile and turns quickly. Don't be surprised if a short-term rally begins after the bottoming action.

Rules for Crude Oil Trade #3:

1. Enters short February Crude Oil from the first trading day after October 11th through the first trading day of December.

2. Place a short entry stop 1 tick (0.01 dollars) below the low of the last 12 trading days. Move the entry stop as the 12-day low changes.

3. Place a protective stop 1 tick (0.01 dollars) above the high of the last 4 trading days. **Note**: This protective stop **does not change** until it is replaced by the trailing profit stop.

4. When the high of the last 15 trading days is equal to or less than the entry price, move the stop down to 1 tick (0.01 dollars) above the 15-day high. As the 15-day high decreases, this stop price is lowered.

5. If stopped out while still in the trade entry window, go back to #2 and enter new entry orders.

6. Exit this trade on the close of the first trading day after December 19th.

Historical Results of Crude Oil Trade #3
February (G) Crude Oil

CL		ENTRY DATE	L / S	ENTRY PRICE	EXIT DATE	EXIT METHOD	EXIT PRICE	TRADE P/L	YEARLY P/L
1984	G	11/10/83	S	29.94	12/20/83	DATEX	28.76	$1,180	$1,180
1985	G	10/12/84	S	29.26	12/20/84	DATEX	26.33	$2,930	$2,930
1986	G	12/02/85	S	28.50	12/20/85	DATEX	25.77	$2,730	$2,730
1987	G	10/28/86	S	14.34	10/31/86	PROT	15.81	-$1,470	
	G	11/24/86	S	15.24	12/11/86	PROT	15.77	-$530	-$2,000
1988	G	11/02/87	S	19.47	12/21/87	DATEX	15.40	$4,070	$4,070
1989	G	11/17/88	S	13.25	11/23/88	PROT	14.15	-$900	-$900
1990	G	10/26/89	S	19.22	12/01/89	PROT	20.01	-$790	-$790
1991	G	10/18/90	S	31.12	12/20/90	DATEX	26.39	$4,730	$4,730
1992	G	11/11/91	S	22.51	12/20/91	DATEX	18.52	$3,990	$3,990
1993	G	10/21/92	S	21.45	12/21/92	DATEX	19.98	$1,470	$1,470
1994	G	10/15/93	S	18.59	12/20/93	DATEX	14.38	$4,210	$4,210
1995	G	10/12/94	S	17.76	12/20/94	DATEX	17.02	$740	$740
1996		N/T							
1997	G	10/30/96	S	23.29	12/02/96	PROT	24.29	-$1,000	-$1,000
1998	G	10/17/97	S	20.59	12/22/97	DATEX	18.32	$2,270	$2,270
1999	G	10/13/98	S	14.74	12/21/98	DATEX	11.02	$3,720	$3,720
2000		N/T							
2001	G	10/27/00	S	30.90	11/14/00	PROT	32.79	-$1,890	
	G	12/01/00	S	32.19	12/20/00	DATEX	25.77	$6,420	$4,530
2002	G	10/18/01	S	21.79	12/20/01	DATEX	19.28	$2,510	$2,510
2003	G	10/21/02	S	27.99	11/22/02	PS	26.67	$1,320	$1,320

EXIT LEGEND:
DATEX = Exit Date
PROT = Protective Stop
PS = Profit Stop
REV = Reverse Entry

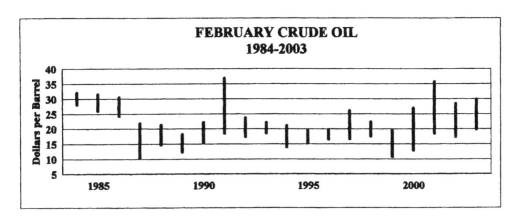

February Crude Oil has both a well defined top around the $35 a barrel price and a well defined bottom area at $11 to $12 a barrel. The lowest entry price for Crude Oil Trade #3 that produced profits was just below the $15 area. I surely would skip any entry below $10. It might be profitable but not a home run.

- Chapter 9 -

HEATING OIL

Product Information:

Heating Oil is one of the many products distilled from crude oil. Crude oil is distilled ("fractionalized") in tall metal towers in refineries. The crude oil is heated and fed into the bottom of the tower. The heating causes the various products to divide into liquids of varying densities. The lighter density products, butane, gasoline and kerosene, rise to the top. The heavier density liquids, heating oil and diesel oil, sink to the bottom of the tower.

Market Information:

The New York Mercantile Exchange began trading Heating Oil futures contracts (42,000 gallons) in 1978, five years before Crude Oil futures. The trading symbol is "HO." Heating Oil contract months comprise all months of the year. In 1987, they began trading options on the futures.

Demand Information:

The Heating Oil market is inelastic. Nobody wants to sit in a cold house during the winter. The only real variation in demand will be the weather conditions in the Northeastern United States, where heating oil is used to heat most homes.

Supply Information:

The refineries control the production of heating oil. During late summer and fall, the refineries concentrate on the production of heating oil, both to sell immediately and to build up their supplies should the winter be long and hard.

Reports:

American Petroleum Industry's Weekly Report

HEATING OIL TRADE #1

Fundamental Commentary:

Heating Oil, one of the two major products from the refining of crude oil, is used to heat homes, mostly in the northeastern United States. The companies that supply heating oil to their residential and business customers order bulk heating oil early so that they can fill orders before the beginning of winter. As the winter drags on, the supply is used up. Should the winter be especially long and cold, the customers' tanks need to be refilled and demand on the refineries increases. This increase in demand propels the price of heating oil upward. Heating Oil Trade #1 takes full advantage of this rally.

Performance History

1980-2002

Total Years Examined	23	
Profitable Years	12	(75%)
Losing Years	4	(25%)
Inactive Years	7	

1980-2002

Total Net Profit	$25,423
Average Profit	$2,418
Average Loss	$899
Profit-to-Loss Ratio	2.7
Total Profits/Total Losses	8.1
Average Yearly "SUMM" Percent Profit	7.9%
Home Run Percentage	18.8%

Performance Commentary:

This is a very good trade. The high profitability (75%) combined with the rather low average loss ($899) and high average profit ($2418) makes this trade one to be watched every year.

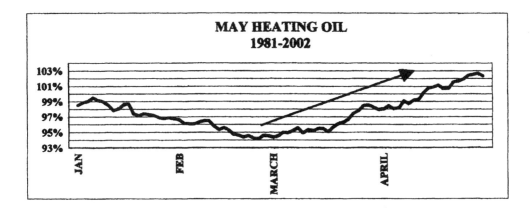

Chart Comments:

Set-up:

There are two very profitable bottom formations that should be watched for in May Heating Oil. The first and by far the most profitable is when the market, after a long downtrend, suddenly makes a major low, reverses and begins to rally. This most often happens in February. The second pattern is actually a version of the first. The market has a long downtrend and forms a bottoming consolidation range. After forming this range the market attempts to make a new major low, but fails, and begins to trend upwards. This second bottom also happens in or near the month of February. Watch for these patterns as a major rally usually follows. Heating Oil Trade #1 catches this rally.

After Entry:

After entering the trade expect a few days to a week of price consolidation after which the rally continues. Rarely does this consolidation stop out the trade. If it does, enter new orders immediately.

Topping:

If the decline from the December-January highs is moderate, new highs can be expected. If, on the other hand, the decline from the highs was steep, the rally will not penetrate the old highs.

Rules for Heating Oil Trade #1:

1. Enters long May Heating Oil from the first trading day after February 24th through the first trading day of April.

2. Place a long entry stop 1 tick (0.01 cents) above the high of the last 23 trading days. Move the entry stop as the 23-day high changes.

3. Place a protective stop 1 tick (0.01 cents) below the low of the last 2 trading days. **Note**: This protective stop **does not change** until it is replaced by the trailing profit stop.

4. When the low of the last 9 trading days is equal to or greater than the entry price, move the stop up to 1 tick (0.01 cents) below the 9-day low. As the 9-day low increases, this stop price is raised.

5. If stopped out while still in the trade entry window, go back to #2 and enter new entry orders.

6. Exit this trade on the close of the first trading day after April 20th.

Historical Results of Heating Oil Trade #1
May (K) Heating Oil

HO		ENTRY DATE	L/S	ENTRY PRICE	EXIT DATE	EXIT METHOD	EXIT PRICE	TRADE P/L	YEARLY P/L
1980		N/T							
1981		N/T							
1982	K	03/31/82	L	78.00	04/21/82	DATEX	88.36	$4,351	$4,351
1983	K	03/22/83	L	73.01	04/21/83	DATEX	82.72	$4,078	$4,078
1984	K	02/27/84	L	77.41	04/23/84	DATEX	82.83	$2,276	$2,276
1985	K	03/04/85	L	70.31	04/11/85	PS	75.01	$1,974	$1,974
1986		N/T							
1987	K	03/16/87	L	49.61	03/19/87	PROT	48.19	-$596	-$596
1988	K	03/23/88	L	44.91	04/21/88	DATEX	50.54	$2,365	$2,365
1989	K	02/27/89	L	48.25	04/05/89	PS	52.31	$1,705	$1,705
1990		N/T							
1991	K	03/20/91	L	55.51	04/22/91	DATEX	57.23	$722	$722
1992	K	03/20/92	L	53.71	03/20/92	PROT	52.49	-$512	
	K	04/01/92	L	53.81	04/21/92	DATEX	57.36	$1,491	$979
1993	K	02/25/93	L	57.70	03/11/93	PROT	56.44	-$529	-$529
1994	K	04/04/94	L	44.46	04/21/94	DATEX	46.87	$1,012	$1,012
1995		N/T							
1996	K	03/13/96	L	51.76	04/17/96	PS	58.11	$2,667	$2,667
1997		N/T							
1998	K	03/23/98	L	47.50	04/21/98	DATEX	44.04	-$1,453	-$1,453
1999	K	03/04/99	L	34.71	04/21/99	DATEX	43.70	$3,776	$3,776
2000	K	02/25/00	L	70.81	03/15/00	PROT	68.39	-$1,016	-$1,016
2001		N/T							
2002	K	03/01/02	L	58.20	04/11/02	PS	65.61	$3,112	$3,112

EXIT LEGEND:
DATEX = Exit Date
PROT = Protective Stop
PS = Profit Stop
REV = Reverse Entry

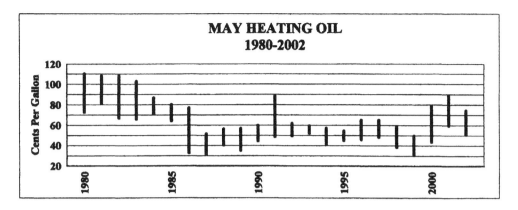

May Heating Oil has a well defined and strong bottom on the long-term chart at 30 cents per gallon. The top range is less well defined at around the 80 cent per gallon price. Heating Oil Trade #1 has never entered above 80 cents but has ridden an uptrend into the upper eighties. Instead of skipping trades above 80, I'd take the trade and then watch as the price increases. The oils can be explosive at times.

HEATING OIL TRADE #2

Fundamental Commentary:

In the late summer and early fall, oil refineries receive piles of orders from local heating oil distributors. The cold weather will come soon and they need to have a large supply on hand. As these orders are received, the refineries attempt to fill them from the supply they have on hand. Often the demand outweighs the supply and prices rally. Remember, for the last few months the refineries have been concentrating on the production of gasoline for the ongoing driving season. Heating Oil Trade #2 jumps on this uptrend to earn super profits.

Performance History

1980-2002

Total Years Examined	23	
Profitable Years	18	(78%)
Losing Years	5	(22%)
Inactive Years	0	

1980-2002

Total Net Profit	$46,685
Average Profit	$2,917
Average Loss	$1,162
Profit-to-Loss Ratio	2.5
Total Profits/Total Losses	9
Average Yearly "SUMM" Percent Profit	8.8%
Home Run Percentage	17.4%

Performance Commentary:

This trade has a long history of producing profits, and good Profit-to-Loss and Total Profits/Total Losses ratios. The Home Run Percentage (17.4%) isn't bad either. Watch this trade, at times prices and profits can really soar!

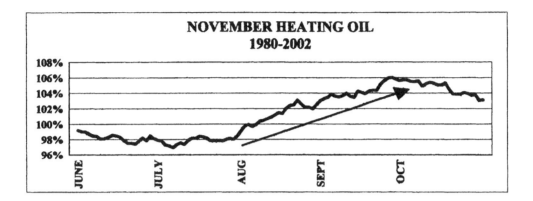

Chart Comments:

Set-up:

After a long-term downtrend, November Heating Oil should bottom out in a "V" pattern anytime from early June to mid-July. About one third of the time the bottom does not come until August. The earlier the bottom, the greater the potential profit. This is not to say that trades entered after later bottoms aren't profitable. They are.

After Entry:

Better than half of the trades entered show a paper profit early, regardless of the timing of the bottom. Others back and fill. Occasionally the first entry is stopped out. If the first entry is a loss, the second has been profitable 75% of the time.

Topping:

This trade tops out in mid-September to early October, after prices begin to struggle to make new highs. Often the market will make a new high, fall back for a few days and make another new high. This new high will not be that much higher than the last one. This is an excellent sign that the market is running out of steam and forming a top.

Rules for Heating Oil Trade #2:

1. Enters long November Heating Oil from the second trading day of July through the last trading day of September.

2. Place a long entry stop 1 tick (0.01 cents) above the high of the last 19 trading days. Move the entry stop as the 19-day high changes.

3. Place a protective stop 1 tick (0.01 cents) under the low of the last 5 trading days. **Note**: This protective stop **does not change** until it is replaced by the trailing profit stop.

4. When the low of the last 11 trading days is equal to or greater than the entry price, move the stop up to 1 tick (0.01 cents) below the 11-day low. As the 11-day low increases, this stop price is raised.

5. If stopped out while still in the trade entry window, go back to #2 and enter new entry orders.

6. Exit this trade on the close of the first trading day after October 8th.

Historical Results of Heating Oil Trade #2
November (X) Heating Oil

HO		ENTRY DATE	L / S	ENTRY PRICE	EXIT DATE	EXIT METHOD	EXIT PRICE	TRADE P/L	YEARLY P/L
1980	X	09/03/80	L	78.91	10/09/80	DATEX	80.50	$668	$668
1981	X	07/06/81	L	96.81	08/10/81	PS	97.78	$407	
	X	08/20/81	L	99.60	08/21/81	PROT	97.74	-$781	
	X	09/24/81	L	96.51	10/09/81	DATEX	98.38	$785	$411
1982	X	08/09/82	L	91.81	10/11/82	DATEX	100.85	$3,797	$3,797
1983	X	07/13/83	L	86.01	08/22/83	PS	86.69	$286	$286
1984	X	08/17/84	L	80.26	10/04/84	PS	82.19	$811	$811
1985	X	07/10/85	L	71.21	09/13/85	PS	77.19	$2,512	
	X	09/23/85	L	80.26	10/09/85	DATEX	82.25	$836	$3,348
1986	X	08/06/86	L	43.00	09/08/86	PS	44.74	$731	$731
1987	X	07/09/87	L	56.95	07/24/87	PROT	55.79	-$487	
	X	09/15/87	L	53.80	10/09/87	DATEX	55.84	$857	$370
1988	X	07/20/88	L	46.81	09/06/88	PROT	42.39	-$1,856	-$1,856
1989	X	07/18/89	L	53.06	07/28/89	PROT	50.59	-$1,037	
	X	08/21/89	L	53.01	10/09/89	DATEX	58.77	$2,419	$1,382
1990	X	07/12/90	L	53.95	10/09/90	DATEX	106.15	$21,924	$21,924
1991	X	07/02/91	L	59.66	08/07/91	PS	60.74	$454	
	X	08/16/91	L	62.76	09/09/91	PS	62.90	$59	
	X	09/24/91	L	65.86	10/09/91	DATEX	68.05	$920	$1,433
1992	X	08/31/92	L	62.01	10/09/92	DATEX	65.89	$1,630	$1,630
1993	X	08/12/93	L	54.85	09/10/93	PROT	51.64	-$1,348	
	X	09/29/93	L	55.66	10/11/93	DATEX	56.42	$319	-$1,029
1994	X	07/29/94	L	54.31	08/05/94	PROT	52.37	-$815	-$815
1995	X	08/01/95	L	50.46	09/20/95	PS	51.24	$328	$328
1996	X	07/08/96	L	56.11	07/26/96	PS	56.39	$118	
	X	08/02/96	L	58.71	10/09/96	DATEX	73.97	$6,409	$6,527
1997	X	07/02/97	L	57.01	07/10/97	PROT	54.54	-$1,037	
	X	07/30/97	L	57.16	08/26/97	PROT	53.92	-$1,361	
	X	09/23/97	L	55.90	10/09/97	DATEX	60.08	$1,756	-$642
1998	X	09/03/98	L	40.11	10/02/98	PS	41.24	$475	$475
1999	X	07/06/99	L	51.90	08/25/99	PS	55.94	$1,697	
	X	09/07/99	L	59.76	10/05/99	PS	59.89	$55	$1,752
2000	X	08/09/00	L	82.31	09/22/00	PS	97.59	$6,418	$6,418
2001	X	08/07/01	L	75.10	09/18/01	PS	75.59	$206	$206

HO		ENTRY DATE	L / S	ENTRY PRICE	EXIT DATE	EXIT METHOD	EXIT PRICE	TRADE P/L	YEARLY P/L
2002	X	07/02/02	L	71.10	07/09/02	PROT	68.60	-$1,050	
	X	07/10/02	L	71.25	07/22/02	PROT	68.55	-$1,134	
	X	08/15/02	L	72.75	09/03/02	PS	73.75	$420	
	X	09/05/02	L	77.90	10/07/02	PS	78.60	$294	-$1,470

EXIT LEGEND:
DATEX = Exit Date
PROT   = Protective Stop
PS   = Profit Stop
REV   = Reverse Entry

122

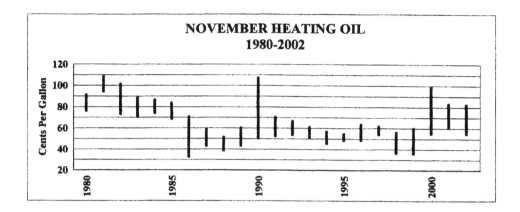

The November Heating Oil chart shows that the 30 cents per gallon price is about as low as prices will go. Because of the timing of Heating Oil Trade #2, no trades were ever entered in this price range. However, if a trade at this point should come up, it looks like it would be a sure thing.

- Chapter 10 -

LEAN HOGS

Product Information:

The hog was brought to the United States by the early explorers. Hogs are an excellent source of meat since they grow rapidly, reproduce twice a year and can be fed on table scraps. All parts of the pig are usable and marketable. It is jokingly said that a packer can sell everything but the "oink." I'm sure that one of these days they will figure out how to sell that!

Recently, small hog farms have been swallowed up by large corporate hog "factories." Instead of small farm herds of 50 to 100 hogs, many of these factories have herds in the thousands. While this makes for excellent economies of scale, it also can cause problems with the local environment.

Market Information:

Lean Hogs futures contracts (once called Live Hogs) are traded on the Chicago Mercantile Exchange. The contract size is 40,000 lbs. The trading symbol is "LH." The contract months traded are February, April, May, June, July, August, October and December. Options are also traded.

Demand Information:

The relative price of other meats and fowl determines the demand for hogs. The higher the price for pork and pork products, the lower the demand (and vice-versa).

Supply Information:

The price of hogs is influenced more by demand than by supply. The inventory of marketable hogs today was decided by the farmer ten months earlier. At that time, the price for feed grain and the price for delivered hogs allowed him to determine the size of the herd he'll raise and have ready to market.

Reports:

Cattle on Feed

Cold Storage

Hog and Pig

Livestock Slaughter

LEAN HOGS TRADE #1

Fundamental Commentary:

A large number of hogs come to market in February, causing a seasonal glut that drives the market downward. In March, the price for hogs drops significantly. The price for hogs may be low, but the pros realize that the hogs still on the farm will not be ready for marketing until after May. This lack of supply creates a shortage, and prices begin to rally. Lean Hogs Trade #1 takes advantage of this pricing inequality to earn excellent profits.

Performance History

1970-2002

Total Years Examined	33	
Profitable Years	21	(81%)
Losing Years	5	(19%)
Inactive Years	7	

1973-2002

Total Net Profit	$28,080
Average Profit	$1,636
Average Loss	$753
Profit-to-Loss Ratio	2.2
Total Profits/Total Losses	10.3
Average Yearly "SUMM" Percent Profit	8.7%
Home Run Percentage	8.7%

Performance Commentary:

The 81% profitable trade expectation covering 33 years, combined with a 2.2 to 1 profit-to-loss ratio, makes this trade one to follow every year. And, since the average loss is only $753, even the smaller trader can take advantage of this trade to build his account.

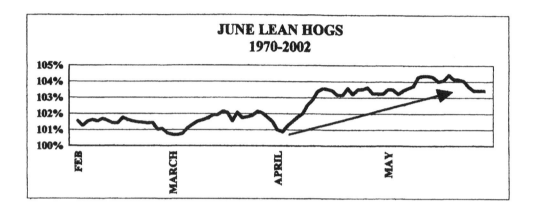

Chart Comments:

Set-up:

Lean Hogs Trade #1 has two chart set-ups. The first pattern bottoms out in December and begins a long-term rally. The second pattern is very much like the first except the bottom comes in February/March and then the uptrend begins. Both patterns are equally profitable.

After Entry:

Don't expect this trade to take off like a rocket. This uptrend is slow and steady. You can expect plenty of backing and filling before new highs are made.

Topping:

May is a pivotal month for the Hog market. Often a consolidation range is formed. In rare cases prices continue to move upward, often soaring during the last two weeks of May. This is just more frosting on the trader's cake.

Rules for Lean Hogs Trade #1:

1. Enters long June Lean Hogs from the first trading day after February 28th through the first trading day of May.

2. Place a long entry stop 1 tick (0.025 cents) above the high of the last 21 trading days. Move the entry stop as the 21-day high changes.

3. Place a protective stop 1 tick (0.025 cents) under the low of the last 5 trading days. **Note**: This protective stop **does not change** until it is replaced by the trailing profit stop.

4. When the low of the last 15 trading days is equal to or greater than the entry price, move the stop up to 1 tick (0.025 cents) below the 15-day low. As the 15-day low increases, this stop price is raised.

5. If stopped out while still in the trade entry window, go back to #2 and enter new entry orders.

6. Exit this trade on the close of the first trading day after May 27th.

Historical Results of Lean Hogs Trade #1
June (M) Lean Hogs

LH		ENTRY DATE	L/S	ENTRY PRICE	EXIT DATE	EXIT METHOD	EXIT PRICE	TRADE P/L	YEARLY P/L
1970	M	03/16/70	L	28.675	03/23/70	PROT	27.700	-$390	-$390
1971	M	03/18/71	L	20.125	05/28/71	DATEX	21.150	$410	$410
1972	M	03/16/72	L	27.625	05/30/72	DATEX	28.150	$210	$210
1973	M	03/07/73	L	37.775	03/27/73	PROT	34.725	-$1,220	
	M	05/01/73	L	37.525	05/29/73	DATEX	39.600	$830	-$390
1974		N/T							
1975	M	03/19/75	L	44.025	05/08/75	PS	46.225	$880	$880
1976	M	03/19/76	L	46.700	05/14/76	PS	49.800	$1,240	$1,240
1977	M	03/15/77	L	39.075	05/31/77	DATEX	45.000	$2,370	$2,370
1978	M	03/08/78	L	49.850	05/30/78	DATEX	54.075	$1,690	$1,690
1979		N/T							
1980		N/T							
1981	M	03/31/81	L	49.675	05/28/81	DATEX	51.750	$830	$830
1982	M	03/04/82	L	53.075	05/28/82	DATEX	62.125	$3,620	$3,620
1983		N/T							
1984	M	03/05/84	L	53.225	04/25/84	PS	55.275	$820	$820
1985		N/T							
1986	M	03/12/86	L	44.775	04/04/86	PROT	42.400	-$950	
	M	04/29/86	L	44.925	05/28/86	DATEX	50.050	$2,050	$1,100
1987	M	03/13/87	L	47.175	05/28/87	DATEX	58.150	$4,390	$4,390
1988	M	03/17/88	L	49.475	05/31/88	DATEX	54.775	$2,120	$2,120
1989	M	03/01/89	L	48.675	03/20/89	PROT	47.525	-$460	-$460
1990	M	03/06/90	L	55.125	05/29/90	DATEX	67.250	$4,850	$4,850
1991	M	03/01/91	L	57.425	05/28/91	DATEX	57.650	$90	$90
1992	M	04/03/92	L	46.775	05/18/92	PS	47.050	$110	$110
1993	M	03/02/93	L	51.325	04/06/93	PS	53.400	$830	$830
1994		N/T							
1995	M	03/09/95	L	46.125	03/24/95	PROT	44.375	-$700	-$700
1996	M	02/29/96	L	53.275	04/26/96	PS	55.800	$1,010	
	M	05/01/96	L	59.975	05/28/96	DATEX	62.850	$1,150	$2,160
1997	M	03/24/97	L	81.000	05/15/97	PS	82.675	$670	$670
1998	M	03/27/98	L	58.725	05/27/98	PS	60.250	$610	$610
1999	M	03/24/99	L	56.675	03/30/99	PROT	52.425	-$1,700	
	M	04/23/99	L	56.725	05/18/99	PS	57.325	$240	-$1,460
2000	M	03/06/00	L	69.525	05/09/00	PS	73.200	$1,470	$1,470

130

LH		ENTRY DATE	L / S	ENTRY PRICE	EXIT DATE	EXIT METHOD	EXIT PRICE	TRADE P/L	YEARLY P/L
2001	M	03/01/01	L	67.500	04/25/01	PS	70.600	$1,240	$1,240
2002	M	N/T							

EXIT LEGEND:
DATEX = Exit Date
PROT = Protective Stop
PS = Profit Stop
REV = Reverse Entry

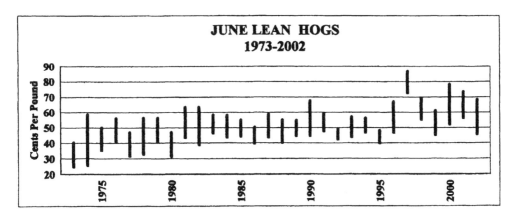

Since the early 1980's, June Lean Hogs have built a strong long-term support at the 40 cent per pound level. Lean Hogs Trade #1 often buys in the 40-50 cent level and earns super profits. For a long time the high range on the long-term chart was in the 60-65 cent level. This level was penetrated when the hog contract was changed from Live Hogs to Lean Hogs in the late 1990's. The upper 80 cent level appears now to be the top of the range.

LEAN HOGS TRADE #2

Fundamental Commentary:

Lean Hogs Trade #2 takes advantage of the rally traded by Lean Hogs Trade #1. After the rally in spring, December Hogs form a consolidation range. The basic question is, has the rally taken prices too high? Most often the answer to this question is yes, and prices begin to collapse. The farmer, who has a little spare time after finishing the planting of his crops, is motivated to move his hogs to the market and take advantage of the higher prices.

Performance History

1970-2002

Total Years Examined	33	
Profitable Years	23	(74%)
Losing Years	8	(26%)
Inactive Years	2	

1973-2002

Total Net Profit	$21,060
Average Profit	$1,228
Average Loss	$674
Profit-to-Loss Ratio	1.82
Total Profits/Total Losses	5.46
Average Yearly "SUMM" Percent Profit	6.2%
Home Run Percentage	14.3%

Performance Commentary:

The 74% profitable trade expectation covering 33 years, combined with a near 2 to 1 profit-to-loss ratio, makes this trade a good one to follow every year. With an average loss of only $674, even the smaller trader can take advantage of this trade to build his account.

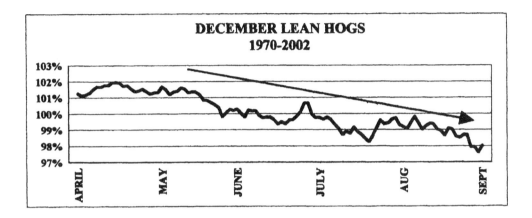

Chart Comments:

Set-up:

From February to May hog prices form a topping consolidation range. Lean Hogs Trade #2 waits for the downside breakout to enter. Occasionally, entry is made during a downtrend from an earlier breakout.

After Entry:

No matter if the entry is right after the breakout, or with an existing downtrend, the market usually forms a short-term price consolidation range around the point of entry. This price movement may stop out the trade. Re-enter a new entry stop quickly, as prices usually break down right after stopping you out.

Bottoming:

The hog market bottoms out in August, forming a price consolidation range around the time of the August Hog and Pig Report.

Rules for Lean Hogs Trade #2:

1. Enters short December Lean Hogs from the first trading day after May 15th through the first trading day of July.

2. Place a short entry stop 1 tick (0.025 cents) below the low of the last 12 trading days. Move the entry stop as the 12-day low changes.

3. Place a protective stop 1 tick (0.025 cents) above the high of the last 5 trading days. **Note**: This protective stop **does not change** until it is replaced by the trailing profit stop.

4. When the high of the last 12 trading days is equal to or less than the entry price, move the stop down to 1 tick (0.025 cents) above the 12-day high. As the 12-day high decreases, this stop price is lowered.

5. If stopped out while still in the trade entry window, go back to #2 and enter new entry orders.

6. Exit this trade on the close of the first trading day after August 22.

Historical Results of Lean Hogs Trade #2
December (Z) Lean Hogs

LH		ENTRY DATE	L/S	ENTRY PRICE	EXIT DATE	EXIT METHOD	EXIT PRICE	TRADE P/L	YEARLY P/L
1970	Z	05/21/70	S	21.975	07/22/70	PS	20.175	$720	$720
1971	Z	06/04/71	S	23.225	08/23/71	DATEX	19.050	$1,670	$1,670
1972	Z	05/23/72	S	26.725	06/26/72	PROT	28.250	-$610	-$610
1973		N/T							
1974	Z	05/16/74	S	29.700	06/18/74	PS	30.000	-$120	-$120
1975	Z	06/27/75	S	46.550	07/23/75	PROT	49.675	-$1,250	-$1,250
1976	Z	06/16/76	S	42.025	08/13/76	PS	39.225	$1,120	$1,120
1977	Z	05/17/77	S	38.575	08/11/77	PS	35.850	$1,090	$1,090
1978	Z	05/31/78	S	49.375	06/29/78	PS	45.875	$1,400	$1,400
1979	Z	05/17/79	S	39.825	07/10/79	PS	38.225	$640	$640
1980	Z	05/29/80	S	38.725	06/10/80	PROT	39.850	-$450	-$450
1981	Z	06/26/81	S	55.175	08/05/81	PS	52.875	$920	$920
1982	Z	06/02/82	S	56.375	06/23/82	PS	56.025	$140	$140
1983	Z	05/20/83	S	44.100	07/21/83	PS	41.175	$1,170	$1,170
1984	Z	05/21/84	S	56.100	06/04/84	PROT	56.925	-$330	
	Z	06/25/84	S	55.250	08/10/84	PS	51.825	$1,370	$1,040
1985	Z	06/20/85	S	47.475	08/23/85	DATEX	38.250	$3,690	$3,690
1986		N/T							
1987	Z	06/30/87	S	44.000	07/01/87	PROT	45.950	-$780	-$780
1988	Z	06/03/88	S	46.025	06/06/88	PROT	47.275	-$500	
	Z	06/14/88	S	46.000	08/12/88	PS	43.500	$1,000	$500
1989	Z	05/24/89	S	45.275	06/15/89	PS	44.775	$200	
	Z	07/05/89	S	42.700	08/04/89	PS	42.775	-$30	$170
1990	Z	05/31/90	S	53.200	07/05/90	PS	53.125	$30	$30
1991	Z	05/17/91	S	47.525	07/29/91	PS	44.675	$1,140	$1,140
1992	Z	05/20/92	S	42.375	08/03/92	PS	40.475	$760	$760
1993	Z	05/28/93	S	43.875	07/02/93	PS	43.050	$330	$330
1994	Z	05/25/94	S	43.775	07/22/94	PS	41.175	$1,040	$1,040
1995	Z	06/09/95	S	42.275	06/15/95	PROT	43.025	-$300	
	Z	07/03/95	S	42.625	07/25/95	PROT	44.025	-$560	-$860
1996	Z	05/23/96	S	53.275	07/02/96	PS	54.275	-$400	-$400
1997	Z	05/16/97	S	71.475	07/01/97	PS	70.800	$270	$270
1998	Z	05/19/98	S	52.975	08/24/98	DATEX	41.900	$4,430	$4,430
1999	Z	05/20/99	S	54.375	06/04/99	PROT	55.275	-$360	

137

LH		ENTRY DATE	L / S	ENTRY PRICE	EXIT DATE	EXIT METHOD	EXIT PRICE	TRADE P/L	YEARLY P/L
	Z	06/17/99	S	52.875	08/02/99	PS	42.875	$4,000	$3,640
2000	Z	05/19/00	S	55.475	05/31/00	PROT	57.425	-$780	
	Z	06/13/00	S	55.875	08/23/00	DATEX	49.925	$2,380	$1,600
2001	Z	05/23/01	S	49.725	06/01/01	PROT	51.875	-$860	-$860
2002	Z	05/20/02	S	39.875	07/01/02	PS	38.225	$660	$660

EXIT LEGEND:
DATEX = Exit Date
PROT   = Protective Stop
PS   = Profit Stop
REV   = Reverse Entry

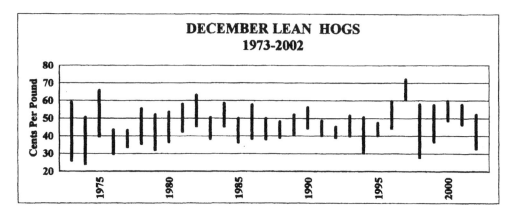

December Lean Hogs have a well defined long range lower support level at 30 cents a pound. It's only been pierced twice since the mid-1970's, and then only fractionally. I would skip any short trades below this level.

LEAN HOGS TRADE #3

Fundamental Commentary:

During the summer a large number of hogs come to market. This drives the price down. Quite often the prices are driven down so low that cash hogs become a good buy for end users. This is when Lean Hogs Trade #3 joins with the big buyers to make a nice, quick profit. Since this trade continues into what once was the delivery notice, it previously was not safely available to speculators. Fortunately, this is no longer the case, since Lean Hogs are now settled in cash and not in actual animals.

Performance History

1969-2002

Total Years Examined	34	
Profitable Years	20	(71%)
Losing Years	8	(29%)
Inactive Years	6	

1973-2002

Total Net Profit	$14,520
Average Profit	$1,027
Average Loss	$420
Profit-to-Loss Ratio	2.4
Total Profits/Total Losses	5.9
Average Yearly "SUMM" Percent Profit	4.7%
Home Run Percentage	8.3%

Performance Commentary:

One of the most important things about this trade is the low ($420) average loss. This allows the smaller trader to join in the game and increase the size of his account.

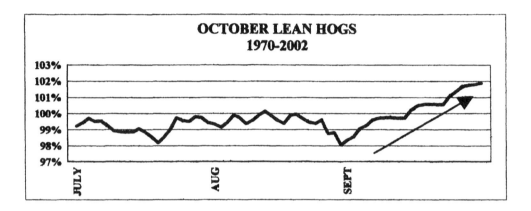

Chart Comments:

Set-up:

If October Lean Hogs made a new two month low between late July and early September, the probabilities are high that this trade will produce a profit. This is the perfect set-up for this trade.

After Entry:

This trade usually shows a profit after only a couple of days to a week. The uptrend is that strong. The big profit trades come after a new low. Trades entered during a pre-existing uptrend are sometimes profitable and sometimes not.

Topping:

This trade attempts to exit during a strong rally. If the rally shows no sign of weakness, additional profits may be earned by tightening up the trailing profit stop and continuing to hold the trade through the exit date.

Rules for Lean Hogs Trade #3:

1. Enters long October Lean Hogs from the first trading day after August 29th through the last trading day of September.

2. Place a long entry stop 1 tick (0.025 cents) above the high of the last 15 trading days. Move the entry stop as the 15-day high changes.

3. Place a protective stop 1 tick (0.025 cents) under yesterday's low. **Note**: This protective stop **does not change** until it is replaced by the trailing profit stop.

4. When the low of the last 7 trading days is equal to or greater than the entry price, move the stop up to 1 tick (0.025 cents) below the 7-day low. As the 7-day low increases, this stop price is raised.

5. If stopped out while still in the trade entry window, go back to #2 and enter new entry orders.

6. Exit this trade on the close of the first trading day in October.

Historical Results of Lean Hogs Trade #3
October (V) Lean Hogs

LH		ENTRY DATE	L / S	ENTRY PRICE	EXIT DATE	EXIT METHOD	EXIT PRICE	TRADE P/L	YEARLY P/L
1969	V	09/11/69	L	24.425	10/01/69	DATEX	26.950	$1,010	$1,010
1970	V	09/14/70	L	19.775	09/22/70	PROT	19.600	-$70	-$70
1971	V	09/15/71	L	18.775	10/01/71	DATEX	20.475	$680	$680
1972	V	08/30/72	L	28.100	09/25/72	PS	28.725	$250	$250
1973		N/T							
1974	V	09/19/74	L	35.975	10/01/74	DATEX	37.800	$730	$730
1975	V	09/03/75	L	56.625	10/01/75	DATEX	64.250	$3,050	$3,050
1976		N/T							
1977	V	09/21/77	L	38.825	10/03/77	DATEX	39.025	$80	$80
1978	V	09/06/78	L	47.625	10/02/78	DATEX	51.250	$1,450	$1,450
1979	V	08/30/79	L	36.775	09/17/79	PS	37.600	$330	$330
1980	V	09/08/80	L	45.425	10/01/80	DATEX	47.775	$940	$940
1981	V	09/09/81	L	52.425	09/16/81	PROT	51.175	-$500	-$500
1982	V	09/03/82	L	63.825	09/10/82	PROT	62.725	-$440	-$440
1983		N/T							
1984		N/T							
1985	V	09/12/85	L	37.325	10/01/85	DATEX	41.975	$1,860	$1,860
1986	V	09/02/86	L	57.975	09/10/86	PROT	57.125	-$340	-$340
1987	V	09/03/87	L	51.575	09/08/87	PROT	50.800	-$310	-$310
1988	V	09/23/88	L	39.325	10/03/88	PROT	38.600	-$290	-$290
1989	V	09/19/89	L	42.000	10/02/89	DATEX	44.175	$870	$870
1990	V	09/11/90	L	50.275	10/01/90	DATEX	56.325	$2,420	$2,420
1991	V	09/06/91	L	45.275	09/30/91	PS	45.725	$180	$180
1992	V	09/02/92	L	40.775	10/01/92	DATEX	42.775	$800	$800
1993	V	09/03/93	L	47.425	09/21/93	PS	48.425	$400	$400
1994		N/T							
1995	V	09/06/95	L	45.825	09/26/95	PS	46.025	$80	$80
1996	V	09/12/96	L	55.100	09/17/96	PROT	54.100	-$400	
	V	09/19/96	L	55.850	10/01/96	DATEX	57.825	$790	$390
1997		N/T							
1998	V	09/16/98	L	42.000	09/18/98	PROT	40.025	-$790	
	V	09/28/98	L	42.275	10/01/98	DATEX	42.550	$110	-$680
1999	V	09/27/99	L	48.000	10/01/99	DATEX	50.375	$950	$950
2000	V	09/06/00	L	54.475	09/07/00	PROT	53.325	-$460	
	V	09/12/00	L	54.550	10/02/00	DATEX	58.900	$1,740	$1,280

LH		ENTRY DATE	L / S	ENTRY PRICE	EXIT DATE	EXIT METHOD	EXIT PRICE	TRADE P/L	YEARLY P/L
2001	V	09/13/01	L	60.775	09/19/01	PROT	59.875	-$380	-$380
2002	V	09/16/02	L	36.275	10/01/02	DATEX	40.400	$1,650	$1,650

EXIT LEGEND:
DATEX = Exit Date
PROT = Protective Stop
PS = Profit Stop
REV = Reverse Entry

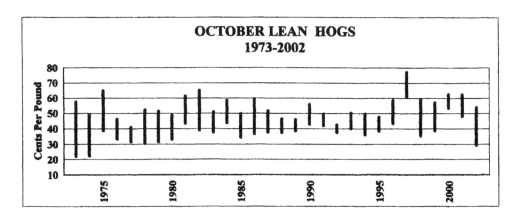

October Lean Hogs have built a long-term consolidation price range between 30 cents on the downside and 65 cents on the upside. Note: Lean Hogs Trade #3 has lost on trades entered over the 63 cents per pound level.

- Chapter 11 -

KANSAS CITY RED WHEAT

Product Information:

Wheat is a cereal crop of the grass family. It has been cultivated for at least the last 9000 years. There are many types of wheat. The wheat traded on the Kansas City Board of Trade is known as "Hard Red Winter Wheat" and is used in the making of breads.

Market Information:

The Kansas City Board of Trade began trading a 5000 bushel contract of Hard Red Winter Wheat in 1876. The contract symbol is "KW." The contract months traded are March, May, July, September and December. Also traded are options on the futures contracts.

Demand Information:

Since two-thirds of the Red Wheat produced in the United States is exported to the Far East, one of the most important factors in the demand equation is the condition of the economies in that part of the world. If the economic conditions in that part of the world are poor, it is very common for the United States to create export programs. These programs help both the U.S. farmer and the countries that receive the wheat.

Supply Information:

There are four major weather fears in the production of the wheat crop. The first fear comes in September through early October, planting time. Hot temperatures during this time can hurt the crop. Second, there needs to be good snow coverage during the winter months. The snow protects the seeds. Third, with potentially the greatest possibility for damage, is during April through June. At this time the crop is in the heading stage, when the crop pollinates. There must be enough rain, and temperatures must remain normal, otherwise the crop may be damaged. And fourth, from late May through early September, heavy rains can slow down the harvest which will cut into yields.

Reports:

Crop Production

Crop Progress

Export Sales

Grain Stocks

Prospective Plantings

Supply and Demand

KANSAS CITY WHEAT TRADE #1

Fundamental Commentary:

Kansas City Wheat, or Hard Red Winter Wheat as it is called, is planted in the late fall. As spring arrives the crop is ready for pollination. This is the time period when both farmers and traders begin to worry about the weather conditions - is it too hot, too cold, too wet or too dry? These fears drive the price of Kansas City Wheat higher. By May, these fears begin to vanish. As the fear vanishes, the price begins to decline. Kansas City Wheat Trade #1 makes excellent profits from this seasonal decline.

Performance History

1976-2002

Total Years Examined	27	
Profitable Years	22	(85%)
Losing Years	4	(15%)
Inactive Years	1	

1976-2002

Total Net Profit	$22,844
Average Profit	$1,102
Average Loss	$350
Profit-to-Loss Ratio	3.1
Total Profits/Total Losses	17.3
Average Yearly "SUMM" Percent Profit	7.5%
Home Run Percentage	19.2%

Performance Commentary:

This is a great trade. The high percentage of profitable trades over a 27-year period combines with a low average loss ($350) and a 3.1 to 1 Profit-to-Loss ratio to make this a trade to follow every year. Considering the average length of this trade, about 6 weeks, the Average Yearly "SUMM" Percent Profit of 7.5% is excellent.

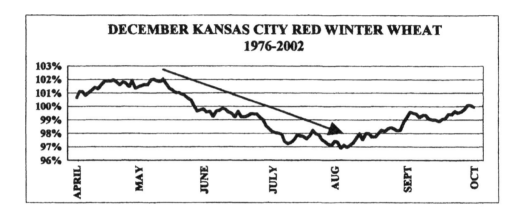

Chart Comments:

Set-up:

Like all the grains, Kansas City Wheat rallies in the spring and tops out between mid-April and mid-June. This creates a wide consolidation range, and is the perfect set-up for the decline that normally follows.

After Entry:

If the usual topping action has occurred, this trade often shows immediate profits. The decline can be steady and at times steep. If the breakout comes very early, the downtrend zigzags and may even stop out the trade. If stopped out, the re-entry is normally profitable.

Bottoming:

This trade bottoms out in a short-term "V" formation that lasts from 3 to 8 days. Ideally, this happens in early August, but at times the bottom comes as early as mid-July.

Rules for Kansas City Wheat Trade #1:

1. Enters short December Kansas City Wheat from the first trading day after May 20th through the first trading day of August.

2. Place a short entry stop 1 tick (0.25 cents) below the low of the last 12 trading days. Move the entry stop as the 12-day low changes.

3. Place a protective stop 1 tick (0.25 cents) above the high of the last 3 trading days. **Note**: This protective stop **does not change** until it is replaced by the trailing profit stop.

4. When the high of the last 5 trading days is equal to or less than the entry price, move the stop down to 1 tick (0.25 cents) above the 5-day high. As the 5-day high decreases, this stop price is lowered.

5. If stopped out while still in the trade entry window, go back to #2 and enter new entry orders.

6. Exit this trade on the close of the first trading day after August 6th.

Historical Results of K. C. Wheat Trade #1
December (Z) Kansas City Wheat

KW		ENTRY DATE	L / S	ENTRY PRICE	EXIT DATE	EXIT METHOD	EXIT PRICE	TRADE P/L	YEARLY P/L
1976	Z	07/12/76	S	386.75	08/09/76	DATEX	344.00	$2,138	$2,138
1977	Z	05/23/77	S	256.00	06/15/77	PS	252.75	$163	
	Z	07/12/77	S	248.50	08/04/77	PS	241.00	$375	$538
1978	Z	06/08/78	S	314.25	06/16/78	PROT	323.25	-$450	
	Z	07/18/78	S	305.25	08/07/78	DATEX	291.00	$713	$263
1979	Z	07/23/79	S	427.75	08/07/79	DATEX	401.50	$1,313	$1,313
1980	Z	05/28/80	S	443.75	06/12/80	PS	433.75	$500	
	Z	07/21/80	S	437.75	07/23/80	PROT	456.25	-$925	-$425
1981	Z	05/21/81	S	463.75	05/28/81	PROT	472.75	-$450	
	Z	06/02/81	S	457.25	07/06/81	PS	449.50	$388	-$62
1982	Z	05/24/82	S	401.75	06/11/82	PS	389.25	$625	
	Z	06/17/82	S	382.00	06/25/82	PROT	391.00	-$450	
	Z	07/07/82	S	378.00	07/14/82	PROT	385.25	-$363	
	Z	08/02/82	S	380.25	08/09/82	DATEX	370.25	$500	$312
1983	Z	05/23/83	S	381.25	06/16/83	PS	366.75	$725	
	Z	07/13/83	S	364.00	07/20/83	PROT	371.00	-$350	$375
1984	Z	06/11/84	S	380.00	06/20/84	PROT	385.25	-$263	
	Z	06/26/84	S	376.75	07/30/84	PS	369.25	$375	$112
1985	Z	05/28/85	S	328.75	06/13/85	PROT	335.25	-$325	
	Z	06/26/85	S	327.75	08/07/85	DATEX	298.50	$1,463	$1,138
1986	Z	05/21/86	S	261.75	06/02/86	PS	260.25	$75	
	Z	06/13/86	S	252.00	07/10/86	PS	245.25	$338	$413
1987	Z	05/29/87	S	282.25	06/15/87	PS	279.00	$163	
	Z	06/22/87	S	271.25	07/28/87	PS	266.25	$250	$413
1988	Z	06/29/88	S	376.75	08/08/88	DATEX	388.00	-$563	-$563
1989	Z	05/24/89	S	431.25	06/06/89	PS	430.00	$63	
	Z	06/07/89	S	419.25	06/13/89	PROT	430.25	-$550	
	Z	07/03/89	S	423.75	08/07/89	DATEX	407.75	$800	$313
1990	Z	05/22/90	S	357.75	06/12/90	PS	352.75	$250	
	Z	06/18/90	S	346.00	08/07/90	DATEX	292.25	$2,688	$2,938
1991	Z	05/28/91	S	304.75	07/12/91	PS	281.50	$1,163	$1,163
1992	Z	05/21/92	S	357.00	05/27/92	PROT	370.75	-$688	
	Z	06/15/92	S	364.75	07/17/92	PS	351.25	$675	
	Z	07/23/92	S	341.75	08/07/92	DATEX	305.50	$1,813	$1,800

KW		ENTRY DATE	L / S	ENTRY PRICE	EXIT DATE	EXIT METHOD	EXIT PRICE	TRADE P/L	YEARLY P/L
1993	Z	05/25/93	S	302.25	06/21/93	PS	300.25	$100	$100
1994	Z	06/21/94	S	339.50	07/12/94	PS	338.00	$75	$75
1995		N/T							
1996	Z	05/24/96	S	620.75	06/10/96	PS	583.25	$1,875	
	Z	06/21/96	S	549.75	07/11/96	PS	523.25	$1,325	
	Z	07/19/96	S	504.75	08/07/96	DATEX	475.50	$1,463	$4,663
1997	Z	05/21/97	S	414.75	06/09/97	PS	397.25	$875	
	Z	06/13/97	S	384.75	07/14/97	PS	361.00	$1,188	$2,063
1998	Z	05/22/98	S	339.25	06/17/98	PS	323.00	$813	
	Z	06/29/98	S	317.75	08/07/98	DATEX	290.00	$1,388	$2,201
1999	Z	05/21/99	S	303.25	06/03/99	PROT	309.75	-$325	
	Z	06/21/99	S	304.25	07/19/99	PS	285.75	$925	$600
2000	Z	05/30/00	S	319.75	06/21/00	PROT	333.50	-$688	
	Z	07/03/00	S	318.50	07/28/00	PS	301.75	$838	$150
2001	Z	05/22/01	S	339.25	07/05/01	PS	322.75	$825	
	Z	07/30/01	S	320.75	08/07/01	DATEX	314.00	$338	$1,163
2002	Z	05/23/02	S	293.25	05/29/02	PROT	300.25	-$350	-$350

EXIT LEGEND:
DATEX = Exit Date
PROT   = Protective Stop
PS   = Profit Stop
REV   = Reverse Entry

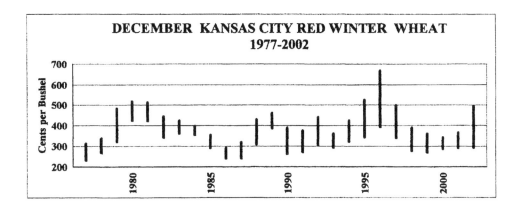

December Kansas City Wheat has strong long-term support in the $2.25 through $2.40 range. If trades are taken in this price range, don't expect home run profits, and watch when prices near the $2.25 range.

- Chapter 12 -

FROZEN CONCENTRATED ORANGE JUICE

Product Information:

Oranges are the most economically important of all the citrus fruits. Under perfect weather conditions an orange tree can be productive for over 60 years. It might surprise you to know that the orange is actually a berry with the tongue twisting name of "hesperidium." In the United States, oranges that do not end up on the dinner table are processed into frozen concentrate. The by-products (peel, seeds and pulp) are used in the production of molasses and cattle feed.

Market Information:

The NYCE division of the New York Board of Trade trades 15,000 lb. contracts for Frozen Concentrated Orange Juice. The trading symbol is "OJ" (recently changed from "JO"). The contract months traded are January, March, May, July, September and November. Also traded are options on these futures contracts.

Demand Information:

The demand for orange juice is nearly static. There is some evidence that demand increases slightly with a good economy and decreases slightly with a bad economy, yet these movements are not significant. Thus the orange juice market is driven by supply, which is totally dependent upon the weather.

Supply Information:

Anywhere the weather is warm year-round you'll find orange trees growing. However, only Brazil and Florida have major processing plants. Weather conditions in these two areas should be watched, especially for early frosts. Frosts can instantly destroy the orange juice crop. Another major weather fear is hurricanes. Many of the orange growing regions are in hurricane-plagued areas. Hurricanes can be just as destructive to the crop as frosts. Clearly then, weather conditions can not only destroy the current crop, but may also permanently destroy the orange trees, thus affecting future production in the area for many years.

Reports:

    Crop Production

    Crop Progress

    Export Sales

    Prospective Plantings

    Supply and Demand Estimates

FROZEN CONCENTRATED ORANGE JUICE TRADE #1

Fundamental Commentary:

This is a classic "growing time" seasonal trade. However, unlike the other "growing season" trades in this book, the weather we are concerned with is in Brazil. Brazil is the largest producer of oranges. Prices for Brazilian oranges rally into May, reflecting the potential for crop ruination by freezing. Usually the freeze fails to develop and the price begins to decline. Frozen Concentrated Orange Juice Trade #1 capitalizes on this downtrend.

Performance History

1968-2002

Total Years Examined	35	
Profitable Years	25	(83%)
Losing Years	5	(17%)
Inactive Years	5	

1973-2002

Total Net Profit	$16,453
Average Profit	$862
Average Loss	$413
Profit-to-Loss Ratio	2.1
Total Profits/Total Losses	11.0
Average Yearly "SUMM" Percent Profit	5.0%
Home Run Percentage	12.0%

158

Performance Commentary:

This is an excellent trade, with 83% profitable years over a 35 year history. One very important point about this trade is the rather small average loss ($413). This is a trade for even the smaller trader.

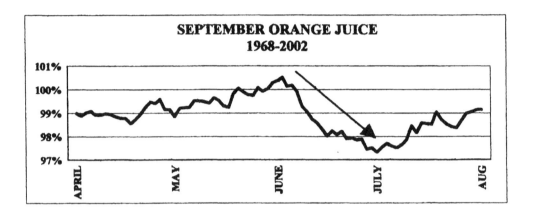

Chart Comments:

Set-up:

September Orange Juice rallies into the May - June time period. This rally can be steep or very gradual. Whether steep or gradual, however, we're looking for a downside breakout after topping and consolidating. If Orange Juice is already in a downtrend, the potential profit is limited by the length and size of the price decline that's already taken place.

After Entry:

After entry, expect a few days of backing and filling. Then the downtrend should continue.

Bottoming:

This down move usually bottoms out in late June to mid-July.

Rules for Orange Juice Trade #1:

1. Enters short September Orange Juice from the second trading day of May through the first trading day after June 15th.

2. Place a short entry stop 1 tick (0.01 cents) below the low of the last 10 trading days. Move the entry stop as the 10-day low changes.

3. Place a protective stop 1 tick (0.01 cents) above the high of the last 3 trading days. **Note**: This protective stop **does not change** until it is replaced by the trailing profit stop.

4. When the high of the last 7 trading days is equal to or less than the entry price, move the stop down to 1 tick (0.01 cents) above the 7-day high. As the 7-day high decreases, this stop price is lowered.

5. If stopped out while still in the trade entry window, go back to #2 and enter new entry orders.

6. Exit this trade on the close of the first trading day after June 26th.

Historical Results of Orange Juice Trade #1
September (U) Orange Juice

OJ		ENTRY DATE	L / S	ENTRY PRICE	EXIT DATE	EXIT METHOD	EXIT PRICE	TRADE P/L	YEARLY P/L
1968	U	05/08/68	S	55.20	05/09/68	PROT	57.65	-$368	
	U	05/13/68	S	54.70	06/27/68	DATEX	44.90	$1,470	$1,102
1969	U	05/09/69	S	51.45	06/02/69	PS	51.00	$68	
	U	06/11/69	S	49.80	06/23/69	PS	49.05	$113	$181
1970	U	05/12/70	S	39.35	06/26/70	PS	36.00	$503	$503
1971	U	06/11/71	S	63.10	06/18/71	PROT	65.05	-$293	-$293
1972	U	05/26/72	S	50.70	06/27/72	DATEX	50.30	$60	$60
1973	U	05/11/73	S	42.25	05/15/73	PROT	43.65	-$210	
	U	06/06/73	S	44.15	06/27/73	DATEX	42.40	$263	$53
1974	U	05/17/74	S	50.10	05/31/74	PS	49.70	$60	
	U	06/10/74	S	48.90	06/14/74	PROT	49.95	-$158	-$98
1975		N/T							
1976	U	05/04/76	S	62.00	06/03/76	PS	60.30	$255	
	U	06/07/76	S	57.90	06/28/76	DATEX	52.25	$848	$1,103
1977		N/T							
1978	U	05/08/78	S	113.75	06/02/78	PS	108.25	$825	$825
1979	U	05/04/79	S	105.25	05/07/79	PROT	107.95	-$405	
	U	05/11/79	S	105.00	06/18/79	PS	99.65	$803	$398
1980	U	05/02/80	S	89.55	05/13/80	PROT	91.00	-$218	
	U	06/06/80	S	89.30	06/23/80	PS	86.05	$488	$270
1981	U	05/19/81	S	144.45	05/29/81	PROT	148.30	-$578	
	U	06/09/81	S	139.05	06/29/81	DATEX	129.55	$1,425	$847
1982	U	05/21/82	S	120.00	06/10/82	PS	119.45	$83	$83
1983		N/T							
1984	U	05/18/84	S	180.50	06/21/84	PS	175.00	$825	$825
1985	U	05/06/85	S	152.00	06/12/85	PS	143.05	$1,343	
	U	06/17/85	S	138.95	06/27/85	DATEX	137.60	$203	$1,546
1986		N/T							
1987	U	05/15/87	S	128.10	06/29/87	DATEX	124.70	$510	$510
1988	U	05/09/88	S	161.10	06/03/88	PROT	165.05	-$593	-$593
1989	U	05/17/89	S	182.25	06/26/89	PS	170.05	$1,830	$1,830
1990	U	06/06/90	S	189.95	06/27/90	DATEX	165.60	$3,653	$3,653
1991	U	06/07/91	S	119.55	06/27/91	DATEX	115.00	$683	$683
1992	U	06/10/92	S	123.40	06/24/92	PS	119.95	$518	$518

OJ		ENTRY DATE	L / S	ENTRY PRICE	EXIT DATE	EXIT METHOD	EXIT PRICE	TRADE P/L	YEARLY P/L
1993	U	06/08/93	S	110.60	06/16/93	PROT	114.90	-$645	-$645
1994	U	05/06/94	S	104.70	05/19/94	PS	99.25	$818	
	U	06/16/94	S	96.20	06/27/94	DATEX	92.05	$623	$1,441
1995	U	06/05/95	S	108.75	06/27/95	DATEX	103.10	$848	$848
1996	U	05/07/96	S	128.45	05/31/96	PS	122.25	$930	
	U	06/10/96	S	117.95	06/18/96	PROT	122.30	-$653	$277
1997	U	05/29/97	S	80.25	06/27/97	DATEX	75.50	$713	$713
1998	U	05/19/98	S	111.45	06/29/98	DATEX	107.70	$563	$563
1999	U	06/14/99	S	86.20	06/28/99	DATEX	81.50	$705	$705
2000	U	05/19/00	S	81.45	06/07/00	PROT	83.55	-$315	-$315
2001	U	06/04/01	S	81.45	06/27/01	DATEX	78.70	$413	$413
2002		N/T							

EXIT LEGEND:
DATEX = Exit Date
PROT = Protective Stop
PS = Profit Stop
REV = Reverse Entry

162

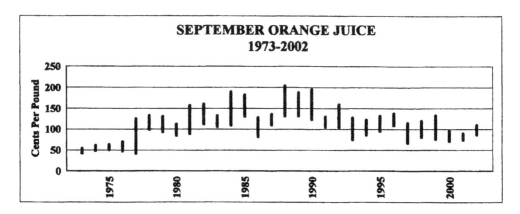

September Orange Juice has a well defined upper range at the $2.00 level and a bottom range around 50 cents. Historically, short trades taken below 54 cents a pound have rarely made money.

- Chapter 13 -

FROZEN PORK BELLIES

Product Information:

Every so often in a movie you hear a reference to Frozen Pork Bellies. Usually the reference is in the context of a joke about commodity trading. So what the heck are Frozen Pork Bellies? Simple, they're bacon. More precisely, the Frozen Pork Belly is a 12 to 14 pound slab of uncured bacon that comes from each side of the belly of a hog.

Market Information:

Frozen Pork Belly futures contracts are traded on the Chicago Mercantile Exchange. The contract size is 40,000 lbs. and the trading symbol is "PB." The contract months traded are February, March, July, and August. The exchange also trades options on these futures.

Demand Information:

The demand for bacon is very dependent on the economy. Bacon can be expensive, and should the economy be in poor shape, buyers will shy away from purchasing bacon. The greatest demand for bacon is during the summer months of June, July and August.

Supply Information:

Since Pork Bellies are produced from hogs, the major supply factor is the size of the hog slaughter. Farmers bring hogs to market if the price of feed is high. When the price of feed is low, farmers hold on to their pigs to increase the size of their herds. This increased herd eventually comes to the market and the price for hogs and bellies declines.

Reports:

Cattle on Feed

Cold Storage

Hog and Pig

Livestock Slaughter

PORK BELLIES TRADE #1

Fundamental Commentary:

More Pork Bellies are moved into cold storage from April through June that any other time of the year. While the amount of bellies available increases, the demand is decreasing. This is the perfect fundamental for a price slide. And prices do slide! Often prices will fall fast and hard. Pork Bellies Trade #1 joins this price slide and profits from it.

Performance History

1964-2002

Total Years Examined	39	
Profitable Years	30	(77%)
Losing Years	9	(23%)
Inactive Years	0	

1973-2002

Total Net Profit	$75,290
Average Profit	$3,863
Average Loss	$1,939
Profit-to-Loss Ratio	2.0
Total Profits/Total Losses	6.5
Average Yearly "SUMM" Percent Profit	5.6%
Home Run Percentage	13.3%

Performance Commentary:

The 77% profitable trade expectation over 39 years, combined with the 2 to 1 profit-to-loss ratio, makes this trade one to follow every year. I would have liked to have seen a higher Home Run Percentage, but that simply is not the way the Pork Bellies market trades. This is one of the higher risk trades.

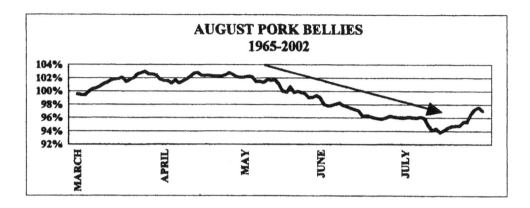

Chart Comments:

Set-up:

The Pork Bellies market forms a long-term topping consolidation range from February through May. Pork Bellies Trade #1 jumps on the downside breakout from this range to make fantastic profits.

After Entry:

Many times this trade shows an immediate profit and then goes into a short consolidation range just below the entry price. The big profits come when prices break out to the downside and begin making new lows.

Bottoming:

The Pork Bellies market bottoms out during August, often forming a consolidation range. The timing of this consolidation range is usually just before the release of the August Hog and Pig Report.

Rules for Pork Bellies Trade #1:

Note: If the volume of August Pork Bellies is low, you can use the following rules to trade the May or July Pork Belly contracts and roll over to the August contract when its volume increases.

1. Enters short August Pork Bellies from the second trading day of April through the first trading day of July.

2. Place a short entry stop 1 tick (0.025 cent) below the low of the last 14 trading days. Move the entry stop as the 14-day low changes.

3. Place a protective stop 1 tick (0.025 cents) above the high of the last 4 trading days. **Note**: This protective stop **does not change** until it is replaced by the trailing profit stop.

4. When the high of the last 13 trading days is equal to or less than the entry price, move the stop down to 1 tick (0.025 cents) above the 13-day high. As the 13-day high decreases, this stop price is lowered.

5. If stopped out while still in the trade entry window, go back to #2 and enter new entry orders.

6. Exit this trade on the close of the first trading day after July 29th.

Historical Results of Pork Bellies Trade #1
August (Q) Pork Bellies

PB		ENTRY DATE	L / S	ENTRY PRICE	EXIT DATE	EXIT METHOD	EXIT PRICE	TRADE P/L	YEARLY P/L
1964	Q	04/23/64	S	$28.350	07/28/64	PS	$23.575	$1,910	$1,910
1965	Q	04/30/65	S	$31.225	05/04/65	PROT	$32.025	-$320	-$320
1966	Q	04/27/66	S	$41.100	05/02/66	PROT	$42.275	-$470	
	Q	05/17/66	S	$39.875	07/05/66	PROT	$41.825	-$780	-$1,250
1967	Q	04/07/67	S	$34.725	05/05/67	PROT	$36.125	-$560	
	Q	06/07/67	S	$40.025	07/31/67	DATEX	$32.600	$2,970	$2,410
1968	Q	05/03/68	S	$36.825	06/26/68	PS	$30.175	$2,660	$2,660
1969	Q	04/07/69	S	$35.675	05/12/69	PROT	$37.975	-$920	
	Q	06/05/69	S	$37.625	07/17/69	PS	$35.025	$1,040	$120
1970	Q	05/11/70	S	$40.375	06/29/70	PS	$36.975	$1,360	$1,360
1971	Q	04/15/71	S	$26.450	05/11/71	PS	$26.025	$170	
	Q	06/08/71	S	$24.900	07/30/71	DATEX	$20.400	$1,800	$1,970
1972	Q	05/18/72	S	$37.500	06/15/72	PS	$35.675	$730	$730
1973	Q	04/11/73	S	$49.450	04/16/73	PROT	$51.725	-$910	
	Q	06/06/73	S	$55.025	06/19/73	PROT	$57.975	-$1,180	-$2,090
1974	Q	04/24/74	S	$45.800	06/25/74	PS	$35.950	$3,940	$3,940
1975	Q	05/08/75	S	$70.575	05/23/75	PROT	$74.625	-$1,620	-$1,620
1976	Q	05/17/76	S	$70.250	05/27/76	PROT	$75.600	-$2,140	
	Q	06/30/76	S	$71.750	07/30/76	DATEX	$65.050	$2,680	$540
1977	Q	05/18/77	S	$57.700	06/29/77	PS	$54.975	$1,090	$1,090
1978	Q	04/12/78	S	$74.925	05/15/78	PS	$72.500	$970	
	Q	05/19/78	S	$66.025	07/17/78	PS	$50.275	$6,300	$7,270
1979	Q	04/03/79	S	$52.325	04/10/79	PROT	$55.425	-$1,340	
	Q	05/07/79	S	$52.775	07/30/79	DATEX	$27.900	$9,950	$8,710
1980	Q	04/02/80	S	$34.200	06/25/80	PS	$35.250	-$420	-$420
1981	Q	04/29/81	S	$55.000	05/22/81	PS	$52.000	$1,200	
	Q	06/23/81	S	$51.025	07/30/81	DATEX	$45.475	$2,220	$3,420
1982	Q	05/24/82	S	$81.125	07/01/82	PS	$74.025	$2,840	$2,840
1983	Q	04/18/83	S	$65.075	06/29/83	PS	$60.375	$1,880	$1,880
1984	Q	04/17/84	S	$67.525	06/11/84	PS	$67.000	$210	
	Q	06/27/84	S	$63.350	07/30/84	DATEX	$51.900	$4,580	$4,790
1985	Q	04/02/85	S	$68.475	05/22/85	PS	$65.925	$1,020	
	Q	06/25/85	S	$63.000	07/30/85	DATEX	$50.700	$4,920	$5,940
1986	Q	04/03/86	S	$54.525	04/28/86	PS	$53.775	$300	$300

PB		ENTRY DATE	L / S	ENTRY PRICE	EXIT DATE	EXIT METHOD	EXIT PRICE	TRADE P/L	YEARLY P/L
1987	Q	05/13/87	S	$65.575	05/28/87	PROT	$69.275	-$1,480	
	Q	06/26/87	S	$72.850	07/08/87	PROT	$76.475	-$1,450	-$2,930
1988	Q	04/08/88	S	$53.075	05/11/88	PS	$52.425	$260	
	Q	06/09/88	S	$50.900	07/22/88	PS	$38.800	$4,840	$5,100
1989	Q	04/04/89	S	$34.525	05/09/89	PS	$32.575	$780	
	Q	05/26/89	S	$31.125	07/31/89	DATEX	$25.075	$2,420	$3,200
1990	Q	05/14/90	S	$61.175	07/30/90	DATEX	$49.225	$4,780	$4,780
1991	Q	04/08/91	S	$59.975	07/30/91	DATEX	$43.150	$6,730	$6,730
1992	Q	04/13/92	S	$33.025	05/07/92	PROT	$34.425	-$560	
	Q	05/26/92	S	$32.100	07/17/92	PS	$29.825	$910	$350
1993	Q	04/06/93	S	$46.025	04/14/93	PROT	$50.675	-$1,860	
	Q	04/19/93	S	$45.450	07/02/93	PS	$35.400	$4,020	$2,160
1994	Q	04/06/94	S	$52.500	06/16/94	PS	$42.275	$4,090	
	Q	06/27/94	S	$38.725	08/01/94	DATEX	$27.175	$4,620	$8,710
1995	Q	04/24/95	S	$37.275	05/23/95	PS	$37.975	-$280	
	Q	06/05/95	S	$33.925	06/08/95	PROT	$36.775	-$1,140	-$1,420
1996	Q	05/20/96	S	$80.125	07/03/96	PS	$76.300	$1,530	$1,530
1997	Q	05/13/97	S	$86.425	05/16/97	PROT	$91.775	-$2,140	
	Q	05/30/97	S	$85.425	07/01/97	PS	$87.800	-$950	-$3,090
1998	Q	05/13/98	S	$51.525	06/05/98	PROT	$56.525	-$2,000	-$2,000
1999	Q	05/17/99	S	$54.825	07/22/99	PS	$39.625	$6,080	$6,080
2000	Q	05/04/00	S	$87.700	07/01/00	DATEX	$83.200	$1,800	$1,800
2001	Q	04/12/01	S	$86.000	05/30/01	PS	$79.850	$2,460	$2,460
2002	Q	04/02/02	S	$73.800	06/14/02	PS	$60.700	$5,240	$5,240

EXIT LEGEND:
DATEX = Exit Date
PROT = Protective Stop
PS = Profit Stop
REV = Reverse Entry

170

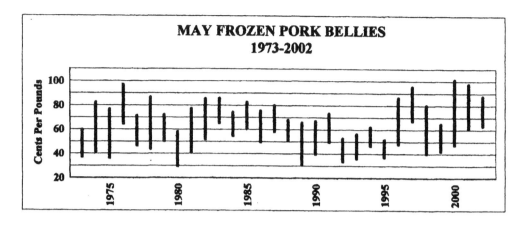

For 30 years, May Frozen Pork Bellies have steadfastly held onto a wide trading range. The top area is around the 90 cent per pound level, and the bottom area is quite firm in the lower 30 cent per pound level. I would avoid taking any short trades below 33 cents per pound.

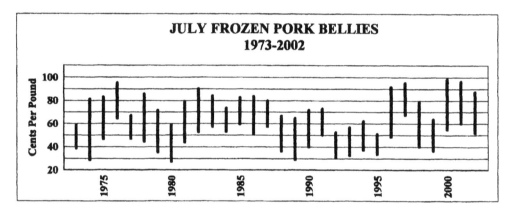

The long-term chart shows that, like the May Frozen Pork Bellies, July has a very defined trading range. Again the 90 cent per pound level is the top, and the 30 cent per pound level defines the bottom. I would avoid entering any short trades in the lower 30 cent level.

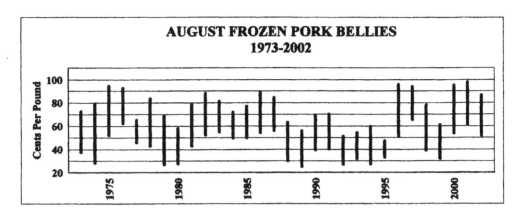

August Frozen Pork Bellies have the same distinct upper range in the 90 cent per pound level. However, notice the lower section of the trading range. Prices often pierce the 30 cent level that held in the charts for May and July Frozen Pork Bellies. Don't be fooled though. As prices approach the 30 cent level, be watchful for reversals.

- Chapter 14 -

SOYBEANS

Product Information:

The soybean is a legume that hangs from a bushy green plant. They are an excellent source of high protein food and edible oil, and are grown in every part of the world where the weather is appropriate. The United States and Brazil are the main growing and exporting nations.

Market Information:

The Chicago Board of Trade trades a "5,000 bushel" futures contract on soybeans. The trading symbol for soybeans is "S." The contract months traded are January, March, May, July, August, September and November. Options on these futures are also traded.

Demand Information:

The major demand for the soybean is in its products, soybean oil and soybean meal. Therefore, the demand for soybeans is dependent upon the size of animal herds (soybean meal) and the demand for margarine, salad and cooking oils (soybean oil).

Supply Information:

Weather is the major concern on the supply side of the supply/demand equation. The crop will be feared lost at least three times during the season. Once, during the planting stage (May through June), again during the blooming and pollination stage (July through mid-September) and finally during the harvest stage (mid-September through late November).

Reports:

Crop Production

Crop Progress

Export Sales

Grain Stocks

Prospective Plantings

Supply & Demand Estimates

SOYBEAN TRADE #1

Fundamental Commentary:

This is a super "growing season" trade. Will the weather be good or bad - too much rain, too little rain, normal temperatures or searing heat? Plus, there's always the fear of an early frost. These are the many questions, worries actually, that only the passing of time can answer. Soybean Trade #1 doesn't really care about the answers. The prices will tell all. And when the prices move, Soybean Trade #1 is designed to jump aboard and ride the trend for excellent profits.

Performance History

1960-2002

Total Years Examined	43	
Profitable Years	31	(72%)
Losing Years	12	(28%)
Inactive Years	0	

1973-2002

Total Net Profit	$82,302
Average Profit	$4,139
Average Loss	$1,843
Profit-to-Loss Ratio	2.2
Total Profits/Total Losses	7.4
Average Yearly "SUMM" Percent Profit	10.2%
Home Run Percentage	33.3%

Performance Commentary:

This is one terrific trade. The 72% profitable trade percentage spread over 43 years is the very definition of a strong super seasonal trade. In addition, the 2.2 profit-to-loss ratio and 33% chance of a home run makes this trade a great account builder.

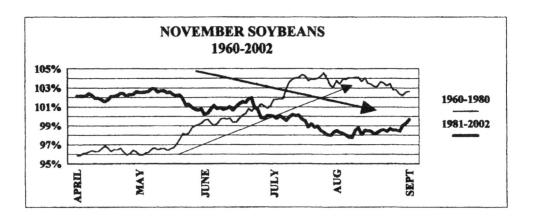

Chart Comments:

Set-up:

The set-up for both long and short Soybean Trade #1 is the same. Expect a multi-month consolidation range from March to mid-May. At this point the chart pattern changes. A breakout on the upside and Soybean Trade #1 buys. A breakout on the downside and the trade shorts the downtrend.

After Entry:

Upside moves are strong and rapid. Limit moves are common, especially in the beginning or the end of the trend. If the market breaks to the downside, expect a slow meandering downtrend. There will be short-term consolidation ranges followed by new seasonal lows.

Topping:

Just as the uptrend can be rapid and violent, so can the top. It's not unusual for "limit up" days to be followed by "limit down" days. This is quite normal for soybean tops, which can come as early as mid-July.

Bottoming:

Soybeans normally form a consolidation range during the month of August. Prices are awaiting the possibility of an early frost to send the market higher. This wait is often in vain

178

Rules for Soybean Trade #1:

1. Enters long or short November Soybeans from the first trading day after May 16th through the first trading day of August.

2. Place a long entry stop 1 tick (0.25 cents) above the high of the last 18 trading days **and** place a short entry stop 1 tick (0.25 cents) below the low of the last 18 trading days. Move these entry stops as the 18-day high and 18-day low change.

3. When filled:

   On long: Place a protective stop 1 tick (0.25 cents) under the low of the last 4 trading days. **Note**: This protective stop **does not change** until it is replaced by the trailing profit stop or a reverse entry stop.

   On short: Place a protective stop 1 tick (0.25 cents) above the high of the last 4 trading days. **Note**: This protective stop **does not change** until it is replaced by the trailing profit stop or a reverse entry stop.

Remember to continue entering the opposite entry orders as described in #2 until you are no longer in the trade entry window. Should you have already entered a long trade via #2 and the short entry price is greater than either the protective stop or the profit stop, replace the protective stop price or profit stop price with the short entry price, thus exiting the current long trade and entering a new short trade. Should you have already entered a short trade via #2 and the long entry price is less than either the protective stop or the profit stop, replace the protective stop price or the profit stop

price with the long entry price, thus exiting the current short trade and entering a new long trade.

4. If long: When the low of the last 9 trading days is equal to or greater than the entry price, move the stop up to 1 tick (0.25 cents) below the 9-day low. As the 9-day low increases, this stop price is raised.

   If short: When the high of the last 9 trading days is equal to or less than the entry price, move the stop down to 1 tick (0.25 cents) above the 9-day high. As the 9-day high decreases, this stop price is lowered.

5. If stopped out while still in the trade entry window, go back to #2 and enter new entry orders.

6. Exit this trade on the close of the first trading day after August 13th.

Historical Results of Soybean Trade #1
November (X) Soybeans

S		ENTRY DATE	L/S	ENTRY PRICE	EXIT DATE	EXIT METHOD	EXIT PRICE	TRADE P/L	YEARLY P/L
1960	X	06/08/60	S	208.25	07/01/60	REV	209.75	-$75	
	X	07/01/60	L	209.75	08/15/60	PS	215.50	$288	$213
1961	X	05/22/61	S	251.25	06/29/61	PS	248.75	$125	
	X	06/30/61	L	250.75	08/01/61	REV	245.00	-$288	
	X	08/01/61	S	245.00	08/14/61	DATEX	243.50	$75	-$88
1962	X	05/22/62	S	237.25	06/28/62	PS	235.50	$88	
	X	07/06/62	S	232.75	08/14/62	DATEX	231.25	$75	$163
1963	X	06/10/63	L	254.25	07/15/63	PS	259.00	$238	
	X	07/17/63	S	254.25	08/14/63	DATEX	251.50	$138	$376
1964	X	06/02/64	L	244.50	06/08/64	PROT	240.75	-$188	
	X	06/29/64	L	245.50	07/13/64	PROT	240.25	-$263	
	X	07/13/64	S	240.00	08/05/64	PROT	247.00	-$350	-$801
1965	X	05/18/65	S	247.00	06/04/65	PS	247.00	$0	
	X	06/21/65	L	248.75	07/09/65	PROT	245.00	-$188	
	X	07/12/65	S	244.50	07/22/65	PROT	247.50	-$150	
	X	07/26/65	L	250.75	08/16/65	DATEX	246.50	-$213	-$551
1966	X	05/17/66	S	277.00	05/24/66	PROT	281.50	-$225	
	X	05/31/66	L	282.00	07/27/66	PS	317.00	$1,750	$1,525
1967	X	05/19/67	L	278.50	06/09/67	PS	280.00	$75	
	X	06/15/67	S	276.00	08/03/67	PS	269.50	$325	$400
1968	X	06/04/68	S	261.25	07/12/68	PS	256.75	$225	
	X	07/29/68	S	253.00	08/14/68	DATEX	252.25	$38	$263
1969	X	05/26/69	S	235.50	07/01/69	REV	236.50	-$50	
	X	07/01/69	L	236.50	07/25/69	REV	234.25	-$113	
	X	07/25/69	S	234.25	08/14/69	DATEX	237.00	-$138	-$301
1970	X	05/19/70	S	256.25	05/21/70	PROT	258.50	-$113	
	X	06/05/70	L	262.25	07/28/70	PS	292.00	$1,488	
	X	07/29/70	S	284.75	08/14/70	DATEX	285.50	-$38	$1,337
1971	X	05/20/71	L	290.25	07/23/71	PS	332.25	$2,100	
	X	07/29/71	S	323.50	08/16/71	DATEX	320.50	$150	$2,250
1972	X	05/19/72	L	325.00	06/19/72	REV	317.75	-$363	
	X	06/19/72	S	317.75	07/03/72	PROT	327.50	-$488	
	X	07/03/72	L	328.75	07/17/72	PROT	317.75	-$550	
	X	07/27/72	S	317.00	08/03/72	PROT	322.00	-$250	-$1,651

S		ENTRY DATE	L / S	ENTRY PRICE	EXIT DATE	EXIT METHOD	EXIT PRICE	TRADE P/L	YEARLY P/L
1973	X	05/22/73	L	516.00	06/15/73	PS	577.75	$3,088	
	X	07/05/73	S	561.75	07/12/73	PROT	628.25	-$3,325	
	X	07/16/73	L	700.25	08/14/73	DATEX	901.50	$10,063	$9,826
1974	X	06/11/74	S	519.25	06/17/74	PROT	540.25	-$1,050	
	X	06/17/74	L	553.25	08/09/74	PS	797.25	$12,200	$11,150
1975	X	05/28/75	S	484.75	06/20/75	REV	508.25	-$1,175	
	X	06/20/75	L	508.25	08/14/75	DATEX	614.00	$5,288	$4,113
1976	X	05/20/76	L	550.25	07/16/76	PS	717.75	$8,375	
	X	07/22/76	S	667.75	08/13/76	PS	645.25	$1,125	$9,500
1977	X	05/24/77	L	750.25	06/13/77	PROT	711.00	-$1,963	
	X	06/13/77	S	711.00	08/15/77	DATEX	506.75	$10,213	$8,250
1978	X	05/17/78	L	630.25	06/07/78	PS	637.75	$375	
	X	06/13/78	S	624.75	07/28/78	PS	611.25	$675	$1,050
1979	X	05/21/79	L	725.25	06/28/79	PS	782.75	$2,875	
	X	07/24/79	S	735.75	08/14/79	DATEX	714.00	$1,088	$3,963
1980	X	06/03/80	S	642.75	06/16/80	REV	665.75	-$1,150	
	X	06/16/80	L	665.75	07/24/80	PS	762.75	$4,850	$3,700
1981	X	05/19/81	S	771.25	06/15/81	PS	771.25	$0	
	X	06/25/81	S	736.25	07/06/81	PROT	759.25	-$1,150	
	X	07/08/81	L	778.25	08/10/81	PROT	722.00	-$2,813	-$3,963
1982	X	05/26/82	S	662.75	06/11/82	PS	657.25	$275	
	X	06/21/82	S	628.00	06/23/82	PROT	646.75	-$938	
	X	07/02/82	S	621.25	08/16/82	DATEX	554.00	$3,363	$2,700
1983	X	05/20/83	S	646.50	06/22/83	PS	632.25	$713	
	X	06/27/83	S	608.25	07/01/83	PROT	632.75	-$1,225	
	X	07/05/83	L	638.50	08/15/83	DATEX	905.00	$13,325	$12,813
1984	X	05/17/84	L	743.25	06/04/84	PROT	724.00	-$963	
	X	06/05/84	S	718.75	06/19/84	REV	755.25	-$1,825	
	X	06/19/84	L	755.25	06/27/84	PROT	705.25	-$2,500	
	X	06/27/84	S	702.25	08/02/84	PS	637.75	$3,225	-$2,063
1985	X	05/17/85	S	582.50	06/07/85	PS	577.75	$238	
	X	07/01/85	S	553.25	07/05/85	PROT	572.50	-$963	
	X	07/12/85	L	581.00	07/17/85	PROT	561.25	-$988	
	X	07/23/85	S	542.50	08/14/85	DATEX	520.25	$1,113	-$600
1986	X	05/28/86	S	510.50	07/15/86	PS	495.00	$775	
	X	07/16/86	L	512.25	08/06/86	PROT	477.00	-$1,763	-$988
1987	X	06/12/87	L	588.75	06/22/87	PROT	558.75	-$1,500	
	X	06/29/87	S	548.00	07/28/87	PS	535.25	$638	

182

S		ENTRY DATE	L/S	ENTRY PRICE	EXIT DATE	EXIT METHOD	EXIT PRICE	TRADE P/L	YEARLY P/L
	X	08/03/87	S	507.25	08/14/87	DATEX	501.75	$275	-$587
1988	X	05/17/88	L	780.00	07/08/88	PS	930.00	$7,500	
	X	07/11/88	S	867.50	08/04/88	PS	867.25	$13	$7,513
1989	X	05/17/89	S	681.75	06/14/89	PS	642.25	$1,975	
	X	06/19/89	L	672.00	07/18/89	REV	622.00	-$2,500	
	X	07/18/89	S	622.00	08/11/89	PS	601.00	$1,050	$525
1990	X	05/22/90	S	624.75	06/25/90	REV	629.75	-$250	
	X	06/25/90	L	629.75	07/11/90	PS	631.25	$75	
	X	07/20/90	S	615.25	08/09/90	PS	611.75	$175	$0
1991	X	06/14/91	S	579.25	07/16/91	PS	548.75	$1,525	
	X	07/26/91	L	570.25	08/14/91	DATEX	550.25	-$1,000	$525
1992	X	06/01/92	L	641.25	06/15/92	PROT	605.25	-$1,800	
	X	07/01/92	S	604.75	08/14/92	DATEX	545.00	$2,988	$1,188
1993	X	06/01/93	S	591.75	06/21/93	REV	611.00	-$963	
	X	06/21/93	L	611.00	07/28/93	PS	695.75	$4,238	$3,275
1994	X	05/17/94	L	635.75	06/22/94	PS	641.25	$275	
	X	06/27/94	S	627.75	06/28/94	PROT	658.25	-$1,525	
	X	06/30/94	S	625.25	08/11/94	PS	569.25	$2,800	$1,550
1995	X	05/18/95	L	607.75	07/31/95	PS	622.00	$713	$713
1996	X	05/29/96	S	759.75	07/11/96	REV	774.00	-$713	
	X	07/11/96	L	774.00	07/26/96	REV	724.75	-$2,463	
	X	07/26/96	S	724.75	08/08/96	PROT	755.25	-$1,525	-$4,701
1997	X	05/20/97	S	688.25	07/15/97	PS	624.00	$3,213	
	X	07/29/97	L	630.25	08/14/97	DATEX	611.75	-$925	$2,288
1998	X	05/20/98	S	613.25	06/17/98	PS	590.00	$1,163	
	X	06/19/98	L	614.50	07/14/98	REV	586.25	-$1,413	
	X	07/14/98	S	586.25	08/14/98	DATEX	534.25	$2,600	$2,350
1999	X	05/18/99	S	479.75	06/07/99	PS	482.50	-$138	
	X	06/24/99	S	461.75	07/20/99	PS	431.25	$1,525	
	X	07/22/99	L	464.25	08/16/99	DATEX	463.50	-$38	$1,349
2000	X	05/25/00	S	549.25	07/21/00	PS	468.00	$4,063	$4,063
2001	X	05/18/01	L	440.25	05/29/01	PROT	426.75	-$675	
	X	05/30/01	S	420.50	06/01/01	PROT	439.50	-$950	
	X	06/01/01	L	441.75	07/23/01	PS	484.25	$2,125	$500
2002	X	05/20/02	L	472.75	07/26/02	PS	518.75	$2,300	$2,300

EXIT LEGEND:
DATEX = Exit Date
PROT = Protective Stop
PS = Profit Stop
REV = Reverse Entry

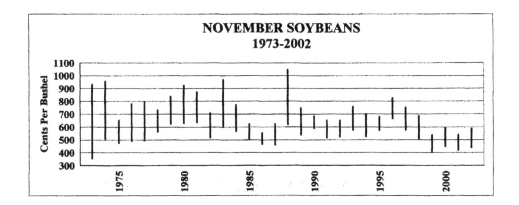

Both the long-term top range and the long-term bottom range are not well defined. The bottom is spread over the $4.00 to $4.50 price level. The top range is even wider, ranging from the $8.00 level to above $9.00 a bushel. By combining the historical trades with the long-term chart, you can see why shorts entered below $5.00 are a bad idea.

- Chapter 15 -

#11 WORLD SUGAR

Product Information:

The commercial importance of sugar dates back hundreds of years. Commercial production in the Americas dates back to the 1600's. The first commercial sugar refinery in the United States was built in New York City in 1689. At that time, raw sugar came only from sugar cane grown in the tropics. In 1787, a practical method for the production of sugar from sugar beets was developed. This massively expanded the supply of sugar and the locations where sugar production was possible.

Market Information:

#11 World Sugar futures are traded on the CSCE Division of the New York Board of Trade. The size of the contract is 112,000 pounds. The trading symbol is "SB" for sugar beets. The months traded are January, March, May, July and October. (Please note that this is #11 World Sugar and not #14 Domestic Sugar which has very low volume.) Options on #11 World Sugar are available.

Demand Information:

Demand for sugar has been increasing at an average annual rate of 1.5%. Demand is closely tied to the economic strength of a country and so will increase and decrease with major economic fluctuations. Neither the advent of sugarless sweeteners nor the warnings of the medical profession have been able to stem the demand for this sweet treat.

Supply Information:

Weather conditions during the growing season and the harvest season are always of major concern. However, sugar is produced from two separate plants, grown in very different climates and harvested at varying times of the year. This means that good weather in one part of the world and bad weather in another can virtually cancel each other out, causing prices to hold in a trading range. At times, good weather prevails throughout the growing and harvesting areas and prices subsequently go down. Alternately, bad weather conditions can dominate both the growing and harvesting areas, driving the price of sugar to wildly higher levels. Both of these weather patterns have recurred periodically for over forty years. It's not unusual for sugar prices to double quickly or, on the short side, decline by 50% or more.

Reports:

    Crop Production

    Prospective Plantings

    Supply & Demand Estimates

WORLD SUGAR TRADE #1

Fundamental Commentary:

Since sugar is produced from two totally separate crops, sugar beets and sugar cane, and the trade is active for five months, there are many fundamentals for this trade. Basically, this is a growing season/harvest season trade. However, the two crops are grown in very different climates with quite different growing and harvest seasons. Often one of the crops is being harvested while the other is being planted. Sugar is a very volatile commodity, driven almost entirely by the production side of the supply/demand equation. That's why World Sugar Trade #1 enters on either side of the market, thus earning profits from whatever trend develops.

Performance History

1961-2002

Total Years Examined	42	
Profitable Years	33	(79%)
Losing Years	9	(21%)
Inactive Years	0	

1973-2002

Total Net Profit	$93,066
Average Profit	$4,275
Average Loss	$761
Profit-to-Loss Ratio	5.6
Total Profits/Total Losses	18.5
Average Yearly "SUMM" Percent Profit	17.2%
Home Run Percentage	46.7%

Performance Commentary:

This is one sweet trade, especially for the smaller trader. Many of the sugar trades require only a few hundred dollars risk and, if successful, often return profits in the multi-thousands of dollars. The trade has a very long history of success and every performance statistic is fantastic. If you follow only one trade in this book, it should be this one!

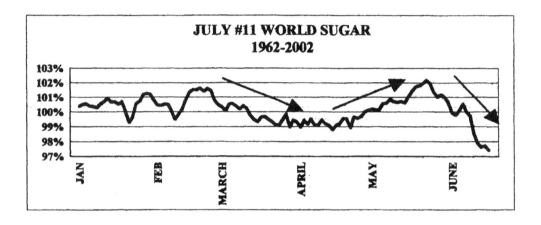

Chart Comments:

Set-up:

There is no real average chart set-up for this trade. Early on (Jan-Feb) the seasonal chart shows no real trend. This is totally deceptive. Upside and downside trends are there, but they cancel each other out. The arrows show the rest of the seasonal story; yet, again, only partially. Many of the greatest trends are countered by powerful reverse seasonal trends. Most important to this seasonal trade is that during this time period sugar is volatile, and the volatility produces profits.

After Entry:

Profits usually come quickly after entering this trade. Sugar tends to trend with a lot of strength.

Bottoming:

It is not unusual for trades to bottom out in a "V" formation and begin a rally. The bottom reflects the previous downtrend. If the downtrend was steep and deep, then expect a quick reversal. If the downtrend was slow, and the price decline shallow, then a longer consolidation bottom should be expected.

Topping:

These trades top out in much the same way as they bottom out, with a little greater expectation of a reverse "V" reversal top. Again, the stronger the rally the more likely a reverse "V" top will reverse the trend. Should the uptrend be weak, a consolidation range will form the top.

Rules for World Sugar Trade #1:

1. Enters long or short July #11 World Sugar from the second trading day of January through four trading days before July #11 World Sugar's last trading day.

2. Place a long entry stop 1 tick (0.01 cents) above the high of the last 26 trading days, **and** place a short entry stop 1 tick (0.01 cents) below the low of the last 26 trading days. Move these entry stops as the 26-day high and 26-day low change.

3. When filled:

   On long: Place a protective stop 1 tick (0.01 cents) under the low of the last 3 trading days. **Note**: This protective stop **does not change** until it is replaced by the trailing profit stop or a reverse entry stop.

   On short: Place a protective stop 1 tick (0.01 cents) above the high of the last 3 trading days. **Note**: This protective stop **does not change** until it is replaced by the trailing profit stop or a reverse entry stop.

Remember to continue entering the opposite entry orders as described in #2 until you are no longer in the trade entry window. Should you have already entered a long trade via #2, and the short entry price is greater than either the protective stop or the profit stop, replace the protective stop price or profit stop price with the short entry price, thus exiting the current long trade and entering a new short trade. Should you have already entered a short trade via #2, and the long entry price is less than either the protective stop or the profit stop, replace the protective stop price or the profit stop price with the long entry price, thus exiting the current short trade and entering a new long trade.

4. If long: When the low of the last 25 trading days is equal to or greater than the entry price, move the stop up to 1 tick (0.01 cents) below the 25-day low. As the 25-day low increases, this stop price is raised.

   If short: When the high of the last 25 trading days is equal to or less than the entry price, move the stop down to 1 tick (0.01 cents) above the 25-day high. As the 25-day high decreases, this stop price is lowered.

5. If stopped out while still in the trade entry window, go back to #2 and enter new entry orders.

6. Exit this trade on the close of the fourth trading day before the last trading day of July World Sugar.

Note: As you may have noticed, the exit rules for this trade are different from the exit rules for other trades. The reason for this variance is that the last trading date for July Sugar varies from year to year. The last trading day has been as early as June 10th and as late as the last trading day of June.

Historical Results of World Sugar Trade #1
July (N) World Sugar

SB		ENTRY DATE	L / S	ENTRY PRICE	EXIT DATE	EXIT METHOD	EXIT PRICE	TRADE P/L	YEARLY P/L
1961	N	03/06/61	L	2.99	06/09/61	REV	3.22	$258	$258
1962	N	01/10/62	S	2.56	02/06/62	PROT	2.71	-$168	
	N	02/06/62	L	2.72	04/19/62	REV	2.60	-$134	
	N	04/19/62	S	2.60	06/12/62	DATEX	2.55	$56	-$246
1963	N	01/03/63	L	4.98	06/11/63	DATEX	10.13	$5,768	$5,768
1964	N	01/10/64	L	10.05	01/24/64	PROT	9.25	-$896	
	N	01/31/64	S	8.39	04/24/64	REV	8.25	$157	
	N	04/24/64	L	8.25	05/05/64	PROT	7.65	-$672	
	N	05/11/64	S	7.10	06/11/64	DATEX	5.06	$2,285	$874
1965	N	01/06/65	S	2.62	01/06/65	PROT	2.75	-$146	
	N	01/14/65	S	2.61	03/03/65	REV	2.73	-$134	
	N	03/03/65	L	2.73	04/06/65	REV	2.48	-$280	
	N	04/06/65	S	2.48	06/10/65	DATEX	1.88	$672	$112
1966	N	01/05/66	L	2.68	02/08/66	REV	2.53	-$168	
	N	02/08/66	S	2.53	06/10/66	DATEX	1.69	$941	$773
1967	N	01/04/67	S	1.45	01/19/67	PROT	1.51	-$67	
	N	01/23/67	L	1.63	03/09/67	REV	1.67	$45	
	N	03/09/67	S	1.67	03/30/67	PROT	1.88	-$235	
	N	04/03/67	L	1.99	06/13/67	DATEX	2.65	$729	$472
1968	N	01/16/68	S	2.48	01/19/68	PROT	2.69	-$235	
	N	02/13/68	S	2.46	05/15/68	REV	2.20	$291	
	N	05/15/68	L	2.20	05/29/68	PROT	2.03	-$190	
	N	05/31/68	S	1.96	06/11/68	DATEX	1.80	$179	$45
1969	N	02/07/69	L	3.23	04/25/69	REV	3.67	$493	
	N	04/25/69	S	3.67	05/29/69	REV	4.05	-$426	
	N	05/29/69	L	4.05	06/04/69	PROT	3.92	-$146	-$79
1970	N	01/13/70	L	3.34	02/04/70	PROT	3.18	-$179	
	N	02/19/70	L	3.44	05/21/70	PS	3.64	$224	$45
1971	N	01/15/71	L	4.44	03/15/71	REV	4.59	$168	
	N	03/15/71	S	4.59	06/25/71	DATEX	4.30	$325	$493
1972	N	01/04/72	L	8.28	03/17/72	REV	8.28	$0	
	N	03/17/72	S	8.28	06/27/72	DATEX	5.97	$2,587	$2,587
1973	N	01/08/73	L	9.11	01/18/73	PROT	8.54	-$638	
	N	01/23/73	S	8.06	02/28/73	REV	8.78	-$806	

SB		ENTRY DATE	L / S	ENTRY PRICE	EXIT DATE	EXIT METHOD	EXIT PRICE	TRADE P/L	YEARLY P/L
	N	02/28/73	L	8.78	06/26/73	DATEX	9.88	$1,232	-$212
1974	N	01/10/74	L	11.65	03/22/74	PS	17.67	$6,742	
	N	03/25/74	S	17.00	04/15/74	PROT	19.16	-$2,419	
	N	04/18/74	L	21.43	06/25/74	DATEX	22.60	$1,310	$5,633
1975	N	01/08/75	S	33.93	06/25/75	DATEX	12.34	$24,181	$24,181
1976	N	02/02/76	S	13.24	02/24/76	PROT	14.10	-$963	
	N	02/24/76	L	14.33	05/27/76	REV	13.89	-$493	
	N	05/27/76	S	13.89	06/25/76	DATEX	12.95	$1,053	-$403
1977	N	01/05/77	S	8.47	01/11/77	PROT	9.08	-$683	
	N	01/17/77	L	9.35	02/22/77	REV	8.75	-$672	
	N	02/22/77	S	8.75	03/03/77	PROT	8.96	-$235	
	N	03/18/77	L	9.36	05/06/77	PS	9.41	$56	
	N	05/06/77	S	9.34	06/27/77	DATEX	7.64	$1,904	$370
1978	N	02/03/78	S	9.65	06/27/78	DATEX	7.09	$2,867	$2,867
1979	N	01/03/79	S	8.74	01/03/79	PROT	8.85	-$123	
	N	01/09/79	S	8.73	02/08/79	REV	8.99	-$291	
	N	02/08/79	L	8.99	03/30/79	REV	8.77	-$246	
	N	03/30/79	S	8.77	06/25/79	PS	8.51	$291	-$369
1980	N	01/15/80	L	17.49	03/13/80	PS	21.57	$4,570	
	N	03/13/80	S	21.57	04/17/80	REV	24.41	-$3,181	
	N	04/17/80	L	24.41	06/25/80	DATEX	33.45	$10,125	$11,514
1981	N	01/19/81	S	27.57	05/29/81	PS	17.16	$11,659	
	N	06/01/81	L	18.61	06/04/81	PROT	16.29	-$2,598	$9,061
1982	N	01/27/82	L	14.21	01/29/82	PROT	13.84	-$414	
	N	02/22/82	S	13.49	06/23/82	DATEX	7.16	$7,090	$6,676
1983	N	01/04/83	S	7.21	02/11/83	REV	7.42	-$235	
	N	02/11/83	L	7.42	02/22/83	PROT	7.19	-$258	
	N	02/23/83	S	6.83	03/30/83	REV	7.41	-$650	
	N	03/30/83	L	7.41	06/27/83	DATEX	11.26	$4,312	$3,169
1984	N	01/04/84	S	8.54	01/23/84	PROT	8.90	-$403	
	N	01/24/84	S	8.19	06/24/84	DATEX	5.17	$3,382	$2,979
1985	N	02/08/85	S	4.72	06/24/85	DATEX	2.77	$2,184	$2,184
1986	N	01/13/86	S	5.77	01/23/86	PROT	6.24	-$526	
	N	03/03/86	L	6.75	05/14/86	REV	7.84	$1,221	
	N	05/14/86	S	7.84	06/25/86	DATEX	5.91	$2,162	$2,857
1987	N	01/06/87	S	6.35	01/08/87	PROT	6.53	-$202	
	N	01/14/87	L	7.28	03/24/87	PS	7.65	$414	
	N	03/24/87	S	7.48	06/24/87	DATEX	6.63	$952	$1,164

SB		ENTRY DATE	L / S	ENTRY PRICE	EXIT DATE	EXIT METHOD	EXIT PRICE	TRADE P/L	YEARLY P/L
1988	N	01/19/88	L	9.76	01/29/88	PROT	9.18	-$650	
	N	02/02/88	S	8.66	03/16/88	PS	8.56	$112	
	N	03/16/88	L	8.65	05/02/88	REV	8.30	-$392	
	N	05/02/88	S	8.30	05/09/88	PROT	8.84	-$605	
	N	05/11/88	L	9.06	06/27/88	DATEX	11.96	$3,248	$1,713
1989	N	01/04/89	S	10.09	02/09/89	REV	10.53	-$493	
	N	02/09/89	L	10.53	03/27/89	PS	11.08	$616	
	N	03/31/89	L	12.58	05/24/89	REV	11.37	-$1,355	
	N	05/24/89	S	11.37	06/15/89	PROT	12.36	-$1,109	-$2,341
1990	N	01/08/90	L	14.04	02/27/90	PS	14.24	$224	
	N	03/02/90	S	14.11	03/05/90	PROT	14.49	-$426	
	N	03/07/90	L	14.95	04/17/90	REV	15.17	$246	
	N	04/17/90	S	15.17	04/25/90	PROT	15.76	-$661	
	N	04/25/90	L	15.91	05/04/90	PROT	15.23	-$762	
	N	05/04/90	S	15.16	06/26/90	DATEX	12.38	$3,114	$1,735
1991	N	01/09/91	S	9.08	03/07/91	REV	9.09	-$11	
	N	03/07/91	L	9.09	04/12/91	REV	8.66	-$482	
	N	04/12/91	S	8.66	06/03/91	REV	8.24	$470	
	N	06/03/91	L	8.24	06/25/91	DATEX	9.96	$1,926	$1,903
1992	N	01/03/92	S	8.41	03/30/92	REV	8.56	-$168	
	N	03/30/92	L	8.56	06/25/92	DATEX	10.97	$2,699	$2,531
1993	N	01/05/93	S	8.39	01/08/93	PROT	8.59	-$224	
	N	01/19/93	L	8.76	01/22/93	PROT	8.61	-$168	
	N	01/26/93	L	8.80	02/02/93	PROT	8.59	-$235	
	N	02/10/93	L	8.99	05/25/93	PS	11.54	$2,856	
	N	05/26/93	S	11.51	06/25/93	DATEX	9.98	$1,714	$3,943
1994	N	01/06/94	L	10.96	01/19/94	PROT	10.72	-$269	
	N	01/31/94	L	11.05	04/05/94	PS	11.87	$918	
	N	04/05/94	S	11.64	05/11/94	REV	12.26	-$694	
	N	05/11/94	L	12.26	06/27/94	DATEX	11.54	-$806	-$851
1995	N	01/04/95	L	15.08	01/13/95	PROT	14.45	-$706	
	N	01/16/95	S	13.99	06/08/95	PS	12.06	$2,162	$1,456
1996	N	01/05/96	L	10.61	01/16/96	PROT	10.42	-$213	
	N	01/16/96	S	10.28	02/12/96	PROT	10.59	-$347	
	N	02/12/96	L	10.64	04/18/96	REV	10.79	$168	
	N	04/18/96	S	10.79	05/17/96	PROT	11.25	-$515	
	N	05/17/96	L	11.31	06/25/96	DATEX	11.91	$672	-$235
1997	N	01/03/97	L	10.94	01/09/97	PROT	10.78	-$179	

SB		ENTRY DATE	L / S	ENTRY PRICE	EXIT DATE	EXIT METHOD	EXIT PRICE	TRADE P/L	YEARLY P/L
	N	01/21/97	S	10.42	02/19/97	REV	10.70	-$314	
	N	02/19/97	L	10.70	06/25/97	DATEX	11.15	$504	$11
1998	N	01/06/98	S	11.50	06/25/98	DATEX	8.22	$3,674	$3,674
1999	N	01/19/99	S	7.47	05/17/99	PS	5.01	$2,755	
	N	06/01/99	L	5.09	06/25/99	DATEX	6.09	$1,120	$3,875
2000	N	01/12/00	S	5.97	03/28/00	PS	5.53	$493	
	N	03/31/00	L	5.57	06/26/00	DATEX	8.57	$3,360	$3,853
2001	N	02/23/01	S	8.49	04/25/01	REV	8.41	$90	
	N	04/25/01	L	8.41	06/25/01	DATEX	9.21	$896	$986
2002	N	01/24/02	S	6.02	03/14/02	PS	5.58	$493	
	N	03/15/02	L	5.65	03/19/02	PROT	5.39	-$291	
	N	04/09/02	S	5.00	04/18/02	PROT	5.23	-$258	
	N	04/19/02	L	5.69	06/21/02	PROT	4.92	-$862	-$918

EXIT LEGEND:
DATEX   =   Exit Date
PROT   =   Protective Stop
PS   =   Profit Stop
REV   =   Reverse Entry

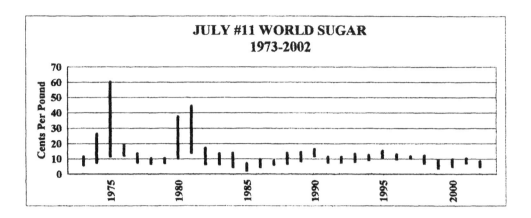

From 1973 to 1981, July #11 World Sugar prices climbed to the sky. Since then, prices have calmed down and formed a more normal range between 16 cents on the top and 5 cents on the bottom. I would use these levels as "no entry" areas. Longs above 16 cents and shorts below 5 cents should probably not be pursued.

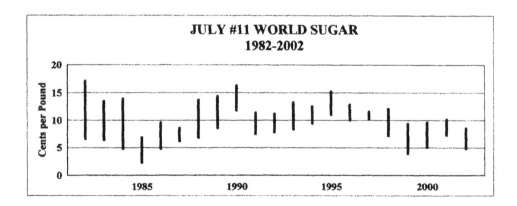

- Chapter 16 -

UNLEADED GASOLINE

Product Information:

Many products are distilled from crude oil. Gasoline is probably the most valuable and most necessary. It is literally the lifeblood of world transportation. As crude oil is heated and broken down ("fractionalized") into various products in the refineries, gasoline rises to the top of the fractionalizing tower. It is among the lightest density of the crude oil products. The gasoline is then drained from the tower and sent to a second refining process, where it is further purified and various ingredients are added.

Market Information:

The New York Mercantile Exchange began trading Unleaded Gasoline futures contracts (42,000 gallons) in 1984. The trading symbol is "HU." Each month of the year has its own contract. In 1989, they began trading options on the futures.

Demand Information:

Gasoline is the most important single product made from crude oil. The gasoline market is totally demand driven. Demand is low in the winter, when the weather is cold and driving conditions are poor. However, when the weather begins to warm and people start going on vacations, the demand for gasoline skyrockets. The refineries had then better have plenty of gasoline in stock to meet this increased demand.

Supply Information:

The refineries control the supply side of the supply/demand equation. While gasoline is produced year round, the spring and summer months put stress on the available supplies. The refineries work at full capacity to meet the massive increase in demand. Note: For quite some time now, the return on new investment in refineries has hovered around 5%. A return this low has limited the building of new refineries in the United States. This points to an eventual under-supply and under-production problem in the industry.

Reports:

American Petroleum Industry's Weekly Report

UNLEADED GASOLINE TRADE #1

Fundamental Commentary:

From March through May the oil refineries are switching their production emphasis from heating oil to gasoline. The gasoline supplies are normally quite low and the strong demand of the summer driving season is on the horizon. Unleaded Gasoline Trade #1 takes advantage of this typical low supply/high demand inequality to earn profits from the coming rally.

Performance History

1986-2002

Total Years Examined	17	
Profitable Years	14	(82%)
Losing Years	3	(18%)
Inactive Years	0	

1986-2002

Total Net Profit	$34,455
Average Profit	$2,568
Average Loss	$498
Profit-to-Loss Ratio	5.2
Total Profits/Total Losses	24.0
Average Yearly "SUMM" Percent Profit	13.6%
Home Run Percentage	29.4%

Performance Commentary:

When you compare the very low average loss of $498 to the $2,568 average profit, and a Home Run percentage of 29.4 %, you can see this trade is one of the great ones. I follow this trade every year and rarely have I been disappointed.

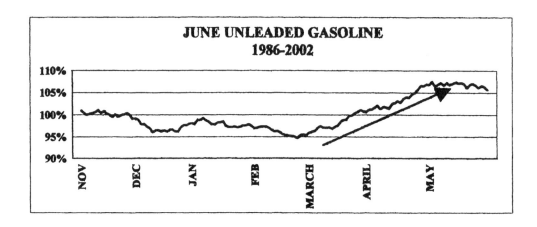

Chart Comments:

Set-up:

Most of the big profit trades have come after heating oil prices made a major decline and bottomed out during mid-February and late March. This bottom is quite often a "V" formation pattern. Trades entered during a pre-existing uptrend have been less profitable.

After Entry:

When this trade is entered after prices have had a steep decline, profits build up quickly. The uptrend is very strong. If entered during an existing uptrend, prices slowly meander upward with a few short consolidation periods.

Topping:

Heating Oil tends to form a consolidation range top from mid-April to mid-May. Many times prices struggle to make new highs and then collapse back into the consolidation range.

Rules for Unleaded Gasoline Trade #1:

1. Enters long June Unleaded Gasoline from the second trading day of March through the first trading day after April 13th.

2. Place a long entry stop 1 tick (0.01 cents) above the high of the last 6 trading days. Move the entry stop as the 6-day high changes.

3. Place a protective stop 1 tick (0.01 cents) under the low of the last 2 trading days. **Note**: This protective stop **does not change** until it is replaced by the trailing profit stop.

4. When the low of the last 8 trading days is equal to or greater than the entry price, move the stop up to 1 tick (0.01 cents) below the 8-day low. As the 8-day low increases, this stop price is raised.

5. If stopped out while still in the trade entry window, go back to #2 and enter new entry orders.

6. Exit this trade on the close of the first trading day after May 9th.

Historical Results of Unleaded Gas Trade #1
June (M) Unleaded Gasoline

HU		ENTRY DATE	L / S	ENTRY PRICE	EXIT DATE	EXIT METHOD	EXIT PRICE	TRADE P/L	YEARLY P/L
1986	M	03/11/86	L	41.35	03/31/86	PROT	37.70	-$1,533	
	M	04/07/86	L	43.50	05/12/86	DATEX	54.10	$4,452	$2,919
1987	M	03/03/87	L	51.01	04/06/87	PS	53.40	$1,004	$1,004
1988	M	03/10/88	L	45.56	04/29/88	PS	50.84	$2,218	$2,218
1989	M	03/03/89	L	54.56	05/03/89	PS	69.09	$6,103	$6,103
1990	M	03/23/90	L	62.81	04/06/90	PROT	61.49	-$554	-$554
1991	M	03/04/91	L	63.50	05/10/91	DATEX	71.21	$3,238	$3,238
1992	M	03/04/92	L	61.31	03/09/92	PROT	59.84	-$617	
	M	03/13/92	L	61.51	03/20/92	PROT	60.09	-$596	
	M	03/31/92	L	61.16	04/13/92	PS	61.84	$286	-$927
1993	M	03/04/93	L	61.25	03/11/93	PROT	60.19	-$445	
	M	03/25/93	L	60.51	05/10/93	DATEX	61.62	$466	$21
1994	M	03/15/94	L	46.36	03/28/94	PROT	45.24	-$470	
	M	03/31/94	L	47.70	04/29/94	PS	48.79	$458	-$12
1995	M	03/20/95	L	55.26	05/10/95	DATEX	63.29	$3,373	$3,373
1996	M	03/12/96	L	58.36	04/17/96	PS	65.34	$2,932	$2,932
1997	M	03/07/97	L	63.51	03/26/97	PS	63.89	$160	
	M	04/14/97	L	61.51	05/12/97	DATEX	64.47	$1,243	$1,403
1998	M	03/18/98	L	49.61	04/06/98	PS	51.59	$832	$832
1999	M	03/03/99	L	41.20	04/08/99	PS	50.09	$3,734	$3,734
2000	M	03/02/00	L	88.31	03/10/00	PROT	84.24	-$1,710	
	M	03/28/00	L	84.31	03/29/00	PROT	81.50	-$1,180	
	M	04/13/00	L	78.01	05/10/00	DATEX	91.20	$5,540	$2,650
2001	M	03/07/01	L	88.71	03/14/01	PROT	85.24	-$1,457	
	M	03/21/01	L	87.71	04/25/01	PS	97.69	$4,192	$2,735
2002	M	03/05/02	L	72.05	04/11/02	PS	78.69	$2,789	$2,789

EXIT LEGEND:
DATEX = Exit Date
PROT = Protective Stop
PS = Profit Stop
REV = Reverse Entry

203

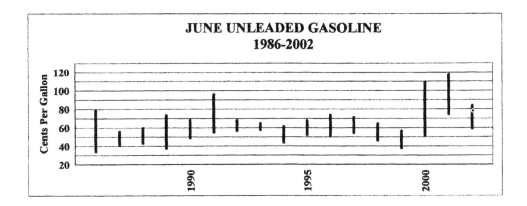

June Unleaded Gasoline has a well defined and strong bottom at around 30 cents per gallon. The top range is far less defined at around the $1.00 per gallon price. I think in time this top will be penetrated, so I'd feel secure in entering the Unleaded Gasoline Trade #1 at above $1.00 per gallon.

- Chapter 17 -

VISUAL CHART DICTIONARY

Throughout this book, in the charting section of each trade, I've used a few terms that might have been unfamiliar to those of you who are new to charting. In this brief chapter I've presented some charts that should help to clarify those trading terms. This first chart presents an ideal visual snapshot of a pattern I've mentioned a few times in earlier chapters.

This chart of September 1996 Soybean Oil, from Soybean Oil Trade #1, shows a perfect upside down "V" top. Notice that the uptrend that preceded the top is quite strong. As I've said before, the topping action often replicates the type of trend that preceded it.

This September Soybean Oil chart shows just how strong a fast uptrend can be, as prices increased here over 30% in only one month. This is typical of a weather market scare. Notice the "V" top, again a reflection of the steep rally preceding it.

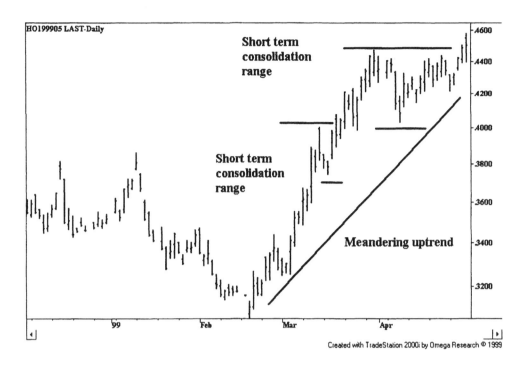

Heating Oil Trade #1's 1999 chart exhibits a perfect "meandering" uptrend. It consists of a series of short-term consolidation periods followed by new highs and more consolidation. Trades like these need patience to hold onto. In the end, it's usually worth it.

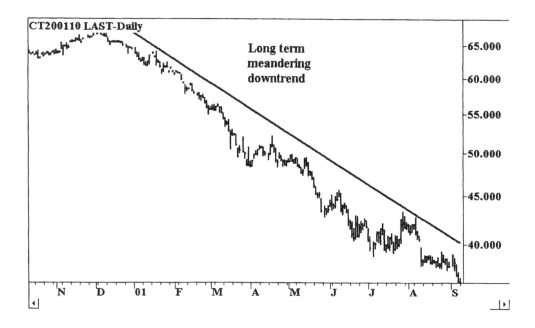

This chart of October 2001 Cotton, from Cotton Trade #1, shows exactly how long-term and meandering a trend can be. Notice that the prices for October Cotton topped out in December 2000. Now look to the far right of the chart. Nine months later, and the price of October Cotton is still declining. These extremely long-term trends are fairly normal for the cotton market. This is because cotton is produced worldwide and not just in a few areas.

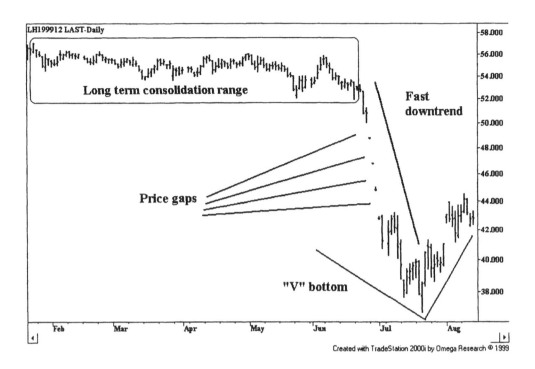

This chart, from Lean Hogs Trade #2, shows a downside breakout from a multi-month consolidation range. The downtrend that followed is very fast, with multiple downside price gaps, and ends in a "V" bottom. Downtrends this severe are rare and usually are in response to a surprise in a government report. The June "Hog and Pig Report" was issued just before the price decline began. The report indicated that there were far more hogs on the farm than the professional trade expected.

This is an excellent example of a violent downtrend (price change) ending in just as violent a bottom. More often than not, the type of bottom reflects the previous trend.

210

This November 2001 Soybean chart shows a perfect multi-month bottoming consolidation range. As mentioned in the Chart Commentary section of Soybean Trade #1, the prices from April-June (planting through growing time frame) are sitting in a tight range waiting for the outcome of weather conditions. In this case, the weather failed to cooperate. It was feared that the poor conditions cut into the size of the soybean crop, and that led to a price rally.

Appendix

CALENDAR OF ENTRY WINDOWS

JANUARY	**Page**		**Page**
New:		Continuing:	
World Sugar #1	187	Live Cattle #1	61

FEBRUARY			
New:		Continuing:	
Crude Oil #1	93	Live Cattle #1	61
Heating Oil #1	110	World Sugar #1	187
Lean Hogs #1	125		

MARCH			
New:		Continuing:	
Unleaded Gasoline #1	199	Crude Oil #1	93
		Heating Oil #1	110
		Lean Hogs #1	125
		World Sugar #1	187

APRIL			
New:		Continuing:	
Pork Bellies #1	165	Heating Oil #1	110
		Lean Hogs #1	125
		Unleaded Gasoline #1	199
		World Sugar #1	187

MAY			
New:		Continuing:	
Soybean Oil #1	49	Lean Hogs #1	125
Corn #1	71	Pork Bellies #1	165
Cotton #1	81	World Sugar #1	187
Kansas City Wheat #1	147		
Lean Hogs #2	132		
Orange Juice #1	157		
Soybeans #1	175		

JUNE

New: Continuing:

    (none)   Soybean Oil #1   49

                                           Corn #1   71

		Continuing	

JUNE

New:		Continuing:	
(none)		Soybean Oil #1	49
		Corn #1	71
		Cotton #1	81
		Kansas City Wheat #1	147
		Lean Hogs #2	132
		Orange Juice #1	157
		Pork Bellies #1	165
		Soybeans #1	175
		World Sugar #1	187

JULY

New:		Continuing:	
Crude Oil #2	98	Soybean Oil #1	49
Heating Oil #2	116	Corn #1	71
		Cotton #1	81
		Kansas City Wheat #1	147
		Lean Hogs #2	132
		Orange Juice #1	157
		Pork Bellies #1	165
		Soybeans #1	175

AUGUST

New:		Continuing:	
Lean Hogs #3	139	Corn #1	71
		Crude Oil #2	98
		Heating Oil #2	116
		Kansas City Wheat #1	147
		Soybeans #1	175

SEPTEMBER

New:		Continuing:	
(none)		Crude Oil #2	98
		Heating Oil #2	116
		Lean Hogs #3	139

OCTOBER

New:		Continuing:	
Crude Oil #3	103	(none)	

NOVEMBER

New:		Continuing:	
(none)		Crude Oil #3	103

DECEMBER

New:		Continuing:	
Live Cattle #1	61	Crude Oil #3	103

CPSIA information can be obtained
at www.ICGtesting.com
Printed in the USA
JSHW010535080120
3441JS00002B/4